How to Survive—
and Profit From—
Your Son's Bar Mitzvah

How to Survive—
and Profit From—
Your Son's Bar Mitzvah

Or Other Significant Event Where
You Are Expected to Pay the Bill

◆

MARVIN SHAPIRO
ILLUSTRATED BY HARRY BRIGGS

SAMUEL
WACHTMAN'S
SONS

An imprint of The Millennium Publishing Group
Distributed to the book trade by Summit Publishing Group

Library of Congress Cataloging-in-Publication Data

Shapiro, Marvin (pseud.), 1941–
How To Survive—And Profit From—Your Son's Bar Mitzvah
Marvin Shapiro
Illustrated by Harry Briggs
96 p. cm.
ISBN 1-888820-00-4
1. Humor
2. Jewish Humor
3. Bar Mitzvah
II. Title.

Cover by Morris Design, Monterey, California
Interior by Cimarron Design, Boulder, Colorado

Printed in the United States of America

2 4 6 8 9 7 5 3 1

Why You Cannot Function Without This Book

This book is written as a survival guide for all you parents who have suffered or are about to suffer through your wonderful festival, whether it be *Bar Mitzvah*, wedding, graduation or wake. *Do not give up hope!* If you follow the instructions given in this book, you will not only avoid the pitfalls and pratfalls of the day, but, in the great American tradition, you will actually end up showing a *profit!*

Several years ago, I read about a unique and special event, the "Potlatch of the Kwakiutls," where a North American Indian tribe had a big bash every year during which everyone gave away virtually everything he or she owned and started all over again—the greatest free garage sale the world has ever known! At several *Bar Mitzvahs* or *Bat Mitzvahs* I've attended over the years, the parents of these young people might just as well have simply called it a "Potlatch" and been done with.

Every year in the United States at least 200,000 Jewish boys and girls reach the mystical age of thirteen. At that age, there has become ingrained in our culture *the* social and financial event *non pareil*—the *Bar Mitzvah* for the boy, the *Bat Mitzvah* for the girl.

The term means "Son (or daughter) of the Covenant" and harks back to a contract between God and Abraham where the Almighty allowed Jews to be the "chosen people" and Old Abe, on behalf of all Members of the Tribe from now to eternity, agreed that male Jewish children would be circumcised at eight days of age. As you can see, that particular Covenant has nothing whatsoever to do with the *Bar* or *Bat Mitzvah*.

Mitzvah has also been translated to mean "good deed" or "good works." By thirteen the "good deed" means that the kid has suffered through Hebrew school (we used to call it *Cheyder* when I was growing up) for the requisite time period set by the local Synagogue Board of Trustees.

Some time during the Middle Ages a great scribe, teacher, rabbi, or social-climbing, doting parent came up with the idea of celebrating the *adulthood* of the child at age thirteen, the age at which, theoretically, the boy becomes a man, the girl a woman, and they are welcomed with open arms into the bosom of the greater Jewish congregation.

As a practical matter, it means the end of getting up early every Sunday morning to *schlep* the kid to Sunday school (or trying to find someone to take the kid to Hebrew School on Tuesday and Thursday afternoons and hearing "Why can't I be like the *other* kids and watch *Oprah?*). As far as the "Son (or Daughter) of the Covenant" is concerned, except for brief visits to *shul* during High Holy Days or involvement in Judaism-by-hormones ("What do you mean you wanna' go out with someone who's not Jewish?"), that's it so far as Jewish education goes for the next several years.

There are similar rites of passage in all religions and cultures. They all come down to the same thing: a celebration where the older generation parts with a substantial amount of money and the younger generation receives a less substantial amount of money and gifts.

I've been through four of these myself. The cheapest was when one of my stepdaughters went to Israel on a Hadassah program and one day decided to take advantage of the twenty-five dollar *Bat Mitzvah* special at the Western wall. I didn't get to go to that one. I will suffer through at least three such debilitating events in the future, provided the younger females in our family take spouses.

My only solace is that eventually my children will go through similar shock, emotional, sociological and financial, when *they* have to shell out the bucks many years down the line. (Unfortunately, no one ever listens to the old line, "Just wait 'til you have children of your own, *you'll* see what it's like!")

The typical cost of a big-city Bar or Bat Mitzvah often exceeds Fifteen Thousand Dollars! Used to be you could buy a house for that. More recently, used to be you could buy a new car for that. I've seen and heard of Bar or Bat Mitzvahs which cost five times as much! I don't limit myself to Jewish rites of passage. This applies in all strata throughout the American culture.

Throughout this book, we will deal with a single event, the Bar Mitzvah of a fictitiously-named representative of the genre, one Herschel Schmendrick Adams (formerly Goldfarb; grandpa changed the family name two generations back).

Let's proceed. It's time to make a killing, both for Herschele and for his parents! (No, it's not a misspelling. Every Jewish mother in the world will continue to call the kid by his diminutive, "Mikey," "Greggie," "Jeffie," etc. even when the "kid's" fifty! I know. My mother still does that!)

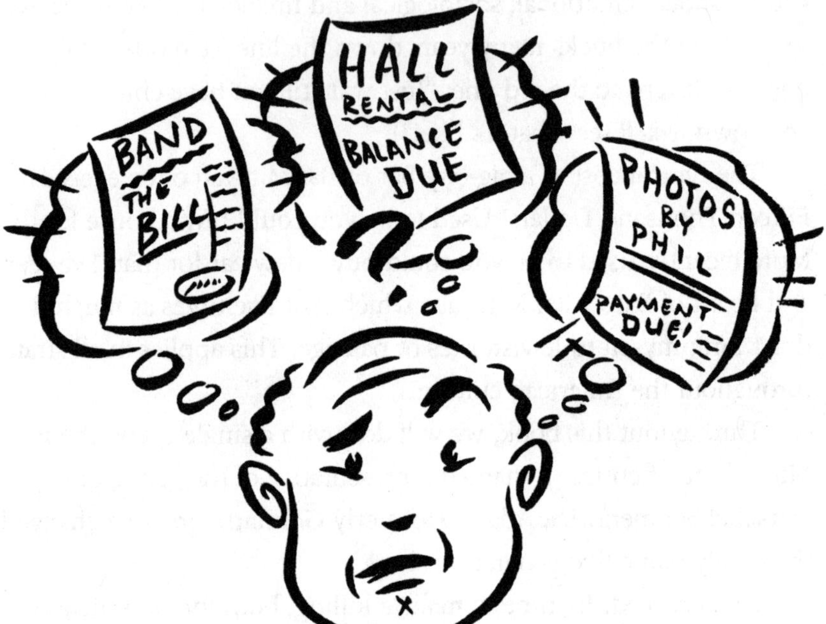
BAND
THE
BILL
HALL
RENTAL
BALANCE
DUE
PHOTOS
BY
PHIL
PAYMENT
DUE!

Why you cannot function without this book

$ **1** $
AN OVERVIEW

Financial organizations use a profit-and-loss statement to determine how they are doing. The income and expense statement of a typical Bar or Bat Mitzvah celebration, assuming 125 guests, looks something like this:

Income	Expense	
-0-*	Invitations and postage	$ 450
	Return postage envelopes	150
	Synagogue rental	150
	Social hall or hotel rental	500
	Food/caterers	6,000
	Band	1,500
	Flowers	250
	Decorations	250
	Wine, drinks	1,500
	Honorarium for Rabbi	50
	Honorarium for Cantor	50
	Furniture rental	100
	Janitorial/cleanup	150
	Videographer for the event	500
	Photographer for the event	1,000
	Programs	Nominal
	Napkins, matchbooks	250
	Custom yarmulkes	250
	Sleeping pills during planning stage	100
	Total	**$ 13,200**

* There will be gifts to the Bar or Bat Mitzvah celebrant, and there may even be donations made to the Synagogue in honor of the event. Never mind the *Yiches* (honor). These don't count for zilch in your own pocketbook.

Not a pretty picture. If your business performed as poorly, you'd be out on the streets looking for a new job.

We must fight the oceans of red ink by constructing a dam. And once we've built the dam, much as they did in Holland, we must plant the recaptured vineyard so we may reap a profit from it. After all, that's the American way.

One caveat: In this book we will keep everything honorable and high-toned. There is no need to do what my *grob* (base, detestable) cousin-in-law Norman did some years ago. He had the *chutzpah* to *sell tickets to his son's Bar Mitzvah* (the cheap scoundrel even charged a premium for the non-folding seats!)

No, we're going to do it clean, even though Norman drives that German car that no Jew is supposed to drive, but all Jews aspire to— the one that begins with an "M" (incidentally, I understand the most successful dealership in the world for that car is in Tel Aviv)—and I drive a five-year-old Dodge. (All Jews are supposed to drive that car because Walter Dodge was Jewish!)

Usually the sleepless nights start four months before the event (thirteen years before if you're the proud mother).

The first and foremost rule for a fun and *profitable* event is you must find as many sponsors as possible, those who will in share in the expense of the venture.

Everyone has a need. For some, that need is to be loved, to be well thought-of, to earn respect. If you don't believe me, listen to Rodney Dangerfield some time.

For others, that need is far more mundane. Forget the talk about honor, it doesn't pay the bills. What's the bottom line?

The key to our line of thought must be, "To each according to his needs," and Karl Marx be damned! Our needs are simple: financial survival is a must. Economic benefit is the goal.

$ 2 $

WHOM DO WE INVITE?

The guest list is the least scientific portion of the program because there are certain persons whom you must invite. Immediate family is a given, a necessary evil. You can bet that some of them will expect to share the naches (pleasure) and the yiches (glory) without a proportionately large gift.

Every family has an Uncle Shmuel who comes to the Bar Mitzvah with a checkbook in hand. He evaluates the decor, the food, the music, and the ambience, and then writes a check in an amount commensurate with the pleasure he has received.

The "have to's" also include the President of the Temple, the President of Sisterhood, the President of the Men's Club, the President of the local Hadassah, etc. We used to be a "nation of priests." Now we're a nation of Presidents. You also have to invite Velvel Cohen, the little old man who sits in the front row and comes to everything anyway; Yenta Levy, who'll spread nasty rumors about you if you don't invite her; and Patsy Saint-Clair, Herschel's ballet teacher (or, you may substitute his violin teacher, piano teacher, or judo teacher, in which case the instructor's name may not be Saint-Clair but Hayakawa).

Assume you've gone through the have-to's and come up with fifty names. Now you shoot for the rest of the guest list. Considerations for sending out these invitations are based on a number of factors:

1. How influential are they? In other words, how can they help foster Herschel's later career?
2. How wealthy are they? More important, how generous can they be expected to be with the wealth they have?
3. What will they say about you behind your back if you don't invite them?
4. How much will they eat?
5. How obnoxious will they be to the other guests you're trying to impress?

In this age of testing for everything from placement in school to placement in the welfare line, you should approach this task objectively. Assuming you can't get a psychological or financial profile on these people from professionals, here are a series of suggested tactics:

1. Ask your spouse (if you're on good terms) or close friend if he/she has any really strong feelings against any given persons. Then make sure you invite those persons. They'll be the "reverse guests of honor" who sit at the "penalty" table. (The penalty table is the one where your mother-in-law, spouse (if you're divorced and not on good terms), or cheapskate have-to-invite is placed. It's usually the closest table to the band.)

2. Ask around the Temple to find out "Who's Who" 'cause you certainly want to be included in the "in" crowd. Invite them.

3. Doctors and lawyers are supposed to have money, but they're notoriously cheap. Do not invite any more of them than you absolutely have to. All lawyers should be seated at the same table. It'll provide a bit of extra entertainment, because it will be like watching a bunch of hens pecking around an empty yard as each tries to hustle the other.

4. Toss a coin in the air, and let it land on a name in the Temple directory. Wherever it lands, that person gets invited.

5. Look up the coming year's calendar of Bar and Bat Mitzvahs. If you invite them, they have to invite you. You'll get a free meal out of it, and all you'll have to do is bring a "recycled" gift.

6. A rather significant rule of thumb: give only token attention to whom Herschel wants you to invite; and take absolutely no notice of whom an older teenage brother or sister wants you to invite. Those will undoubtedly be boys who wear razor blades in their ears, ill-fitting black leather jackets, and hair longer than Lady Godiva. Or girls with orange-colored, spiked hair, dresses up to their navels, nose or belly-button rings, and hip-high military boots. These "guests" will either be doused with the strongest, sweetest, most cloying after-shave/cologne/perfume, or, alternatively, they believe that if they take a bath more than once a year they'll turn to rust, and there's a certain odor that accompanies that philosophy. Besides, unless their parents are invited, don't expect anything resembling big bucks from any of them.

$ **3** $

THE INVITATIONS

You've gotten over the hurdle of whom to invite. The first potential out-of-pocket expense is invitations. You've got to get them sent out and the replies processed.

The traditional way to do this is to ask a friend who's done this before and knows a printer who has a big catalogue of invitations. You go to the shop, bring home five overstuffed three-ring binders and go absolutely crazy finding color-coordinates, wording, and something that's going to be "just a little better" than the invitations used by the friend who referred you. Also, it should be a little cheaper, it won't hurt.

Once you've picked your selection, you fight over it. Herschel thinks the colors are "queer." Little sister Sarah thinks they're "pukey." Older sister Tiffany (a nice Jewish name) thinks they're "rad;" and David, the eldest, doesn't give a damn one way or the other since he just got accepted into U.C. San Diego. Dad shrugs his shoulders and says, "Whatever you decide is just fine with me. I'm only the one who pays the bills."

After the hassle is over, you go out and order the invitations— usually too few, since you pay for them by the piece. Then you go to the Post Office and select color-coordinated commemorative stamps which say "Love" on them. God forbid everything shouldn't be just perfect, right?

Wrong.

There's a much easier, better way to handle all this. Find a sponsor.

Obviously the most responsive potential angel is one dedicated to *youth*. Never mind the local Kiwanis, the Rotary, etc. Their concept of helping *youth* is much too general for us: generic things such as overseas trips to promote international understanding, scholarships, and the like. These don't do you a bit of good unless your child-genius is chosen to take advantage of such a thing (and don't think *that* comes for free, either!). That's not to say you should ignore these noble organizations altogether. Their place will come, just not yet.

No, what you're looking for is a *commercial* sponsor, one that promotes *Youth* with a capital "Y." Go to a high school football game. What do you invariably see? A scoreboard touting *Coca Cola*, *Pepsi* or *Juicy Fruit Gum*—things that Youth *needs*, and *uses*, and *must have* in order to survive! (Translation: be cool).

Take my word for it, a national commercial advertiser's priorities are totally different from that of a Rotarian, Lion or Kiwanian. The big folks in Atlanta don't deal with local events unless they have national prominence. A high school football game is "Friday afternoon-USA." You must convince the commercial advertiser that a Bar or Bat Mitzvah is even more universal. It is linked directly to the *Creator*.

Realize, however, that you can't get greedy about this. If Coke or Pepsi, or even Donald Trump sponsored every single Bar Mitzvah they'd soon be out of business (Come to think of it, Donald Trump may well have sponsored one too many Bar Mitzvahs). So the commercial advertiser should be called upon to play only a very small role in the sponsorship picture.

Next, you must figure out the most logical role the sponsor can play. The answer is simple. Some time ago, *Time* magazine devoted an entire issue to the proliferation of so-called "Junk Mail." That beacon of intellectual enlightenment told us (and remember, if you read it in *Time* it must be true!) that direct mail is *the* advertising choice of our nation.

Voila! The proper place in the scheme of the Bar Mitzvah is to let the commercial advertiser take care of the invitations, the mailing and the processing! The company's completely equipped for it. It doesn't cost the sponsor a dime extra. It's doing a *public service.* More important for your benefit, if someone throws the invitation away and doesn't send it back, you can always say—and prove—that it was sent in the mail, and you have that many fewer people to clutter up the dance floor!

The sponsor no doubt has professionals who design the invitation, write perfect wording which has been cleared by its marketing and psychological departments to insure optimum reception, and color code everything according to the zodiac.

This endeavor must be approached diplomatically, convincingly, and as soon as possible, so that the sponsor has time to pass it through research and development, marketing, budget & financial, and so on up through the Board of Directors. The following letter, or a reasonable facsimile, is appropriate. You may use the model without even giving me credit.

President and Chief Executive Officer
XYZ Bottling Company & Airline
Universal Trade Center and TV Tower
Atlanta, Georgia

Dear Mr. Smith:

More than five thousand, seven hundred sixty years ago the world was created. Shortly afterward, two major events occurred: (1) The groundwork was laid for the establishment of your historically generous and socially-conscious company, and (2) The beginning of our Western heritage took place when Abraham entered into a Covenant with God.

More than a thousand years ago, our common ancestors developed the concept of the *Bar Mitzvah*—an event designed to be high-profile teen-wise—to attract a greater share of the market for XYZ Cola than TV, radio, or media. Your Board is no doubt familiar with this internationally accepted program.

Now you have a wonderful opportunity! With the expenditure of less than one-half of one percent of your advertising budget, you can take advantage of this *universal* marketing opportunity, *and* at the same time demonstrate your social consciousness!

My son Herschel Schmendrick Adams, will celebrate his Bar Mitzvah on January 15, [year] at Congregation Beth Shalom in Pebble Beach, California. As you are no doubt aware, your company controls a [___] percent market share for soft drinks in our area. Your participation in our event will undoubtedly result in a substantial increase in this share.

We are offering you the exclusive license to sponsor the design, printing, postage, and receipt processing for 250 invitations. Naturally, we would not object if you placed an advertising insert in the envelopes. In order to give your message a personal touch, we are enclosing a photograph showing our happy family enjoying XYZ Cola. Should you decide to use the picture for a national advertising campaign, we would be pleased to negotiate for a reasonble royalty. I will provide you with the address of my brother-in-law, who is an attorney, should you wish to contact him.

We are pleased to afford you this exclusive option for ten days. This will give your Board the opportunity to see the wisdom of this bonanza and to send us your favorable reply Federal Express or Express Mail.

Thank you very much.

Sincerely,

Abigail Adams (neé Goldfarb)

You should adjust the wording of the letter to give it a more personal touch. If this same letter goes out to every advertiser, after five or six years, they'll start to see a pattern developing, and they may not be as receptive.

Not only have you incorporated industry "buzz-words" and advertising concepts ("teen-wise," "market share"), and shown that you are up-to-date and "with it," but you have left open the invitation for a long-term relationship, and perhaps engineered a future job as model or junior executive for members of your family. If there are any "long hairs," or outrageous dressers in the family, they must be deleted from the picture. No doubt, the XYZ Company has an image to portray. You must uphold that image if you want sponsorship.

This also assumes that son Herschel does not look like the south end of a horse going north. If the heir-apparent is not the model of youthful exuberance, the situation can still be saved. You create a banner with the name of the company's product on it. If the banner happens to cover Herschel's face…well, that's the breaks.

As you can see, this very simple theory and practice undoubtedly works. More to the point, it gives you the basic, underlying philosophy of running the event to *make a profit!*

**If the heir apparent is not
the model of youthful exuberance
the situation can still be saved**

$ 4 $

THE SYNAGOGUE, RABBI AND THE CANTOR

This presents a bit of a problem, because you might not be able to get around laying out some money. Let's face it, you don't mess with God!

Of these three sticky problems, the Cantor is probably the easiest. Somehow you let the word get out in the community that either:

   a) A record producer and/or
   b) A Hollywood talent scout, and/or
   c) The agent who discovered Jan Peerce and Robert Merrill has been invited to the big event. It is important that you don't tell the cantor this yourself, because that's considered *grob* (declassé). Rather, the word should leak out, preferably from three or more "independent" sources—friends with big mouths.

About two months before the big day, you have a very serious sit-down talk with the cantor:

YOU: "Cantor Levy, I don't know how to tell you this, but my cousin Beryl, who's got a lovely voice, has asked if he could do us a favor and sing at Herschel's Bar Mitzvah. He's coming all the way from White Plains, and I'd feel terrible turning him down. He says he'll do it for nothing, not that it's a question of money…"

CANTOR: "A *cousin*? Why would you want a cousin when you can have a *khazin*?" (This is the cantor's heavy-handed attempt at humor. *Khazin* means "cantor" in Hebrew).

YOU: "Oh, didn't I tell you? How silly of me. He's the Chief Cantor at *Yigal ben Hamotzi* Synagogue in White Plains. They have *Nine Hundred families*. (It's important you use a number substantially larger than the membership in your own *shul*.)

CANTOR: "Oh? (His voice rises with a combination of professional jealousy and professional disdain). And why is it so important you import a Cantor from so far away?"

YOU: "I didn't say it's important to me at all, Cantor Levy. Believe me, it's not. Beryl just looked over the guest list and I suppose he saw some names he recognized from New York or Los Angeles and he called me special—not even collect—to tell me how guilty he feels for not having stayed in touch, and how he wants to make it up to the family." (NOTICE: You *implied* but did not commit to any of the famous agents the Cantor has previously heard about. Let him draw his own conclusions).

CANTOR: "Oho! He wants to mingle with famous people from New York and Los Angeles? And who might they be?"

YOU: (Downcast eyes) "I've no idea, Cantor Levy. Maybe someone he met when he auditioned for Broadway some years ago? For all I know, a movie producer." (Now the hook is really in. Cantor Levy is about to bite.)

CANTOR: "Look, if it's a question of money, I could reduce my usual rate…"

YOU: (Shocked). "Money? Did you say *money*, Cantor Levy? I wouldn't dare think of such a thing. I mean, how many sons does a mother Bar Mitzvah? Money's the least of our worries. Beryl's my cousin, a member of the family. How could I insult him?"

**Cantor Levy dreams of being
the next Robert Merrill...**

CANTOR: "I'm sorry, Mrs. Adams. Please forgive me for even mentioning such a thing. Look, I'll tell you what. Herschel is such a fine young man—truly one of the best boys I've ever come across. Suppose I were to do the service as my personal contribution—as an honor to your wonderful family."

YOU: "Well, Cantor Levy, I'm flattered of course. But what do I tell my cousin Beryl? He'll be heartbroken."

CANTOR: "Look, Mrs. Adams, this Bar Mitzvah is important to me. Beryl will be gone after the Bar Mitzvah. Why don't you tell him he can sing during the after-service celebration? I'll be pleased to help him rehearse, whatever. I could even make a small donation in honor of the boy."

YOU: "I'll have to think about it. I'll let you know next week. You say you'd sing the entire service for free?"

CANTOR: "Absolutely. But not a word of this to anyone in the congregation. This must be a secret between us."

YOU: "I'll think about it."

CANTOR: "Please do. And thank you so much for bringing this sensitive matter to me. I'm always here to help."

So much for the Cantor.

The Rabbi's a bit different.

He doesn't buy into the ego-line. Do you by any chance have a real cousin who could serve as Rabbi for the day?

Assume you don't. You needn't panic. The idea of this book is not necessarily that you're going to get off Scot-free (Oops. I suppose in a book of this kind, that was the wrong ethnic comparison. But as long as we're on the subject, the origin of the term "Scot-free" is Scandinavian!) Just think of the old line, "You have to spend money to make money." If you absolutely can't get out of paying the Rabbi, this may go down a little easier.

But, to use an old Jewish line of reasoning called *"pilpul"* (which, to be honest, I've never heard of except in the Harry Kemmelman books—remember *Friday the Rabbi Slept Late,* etc.?) You can always *try* to be a bit creative.

Usually if you're a member of the congregation, the cost of the Rabbi comes with your annual dues. It's considered "traditional" to pay the Rabbi "an honorarium." Euphemistically, this form of payment goes to the "Rabbi's discretionary fund" or some such appropriately-titled account. Ethics being what they are, the Rabbi is honor-bound to report these honoraria—either they go into a fund, or he declares it on his income tax return.

But a gift. Now that's something else again. Can't be put into a fund. Doesn't need to be declared. Clean for everyone. Thus, instead of paying something as mundane as money, you propose (to your spouse, not to the Rabbi), that the spiritual leader should receive a gift in lieu of money.

The kind and number of gifts one can give a thirteen-year-old boy or girl at a Bar or Bat Mitzvah (other than money, and there will always be some who don't want to stoop to giving such a "common" gift) is limited. The old joke, "Today I am a fountain pen," may be updated to read "Internet subscription," "watch," or even "ball point pen" (*Cross,* of course). You can pretty well bet Herschel is going to get at least one duplicate present.

So what do you do? Embarrass your friend, uncle, or business associate by giving it back? God forbid! After all, an offering such as this costs at least fifty dollars. Isn't it strange that the appropriate honorarium to pay the Rabbi is just about fifty dollars? Then that computer housed in your brain starts working, the gears click in, and *Voila!* Herschel will never miss the gift.

"Oh, ma! Do I have to write *another* 'Thank You' card? It's been a month already, and no one's going to read it. Besides, I forgot what Cousin Shloime gave me."

"Don't give me your lip. Of course you remember. He got you that wonderful [Internet subscription] [watch] [Cross ball point pen]."

"Gee, I thought I got two of those."

"What??? Don't tell me you lost one! You teenagers are all alike. You don't take care of anything, you're always losing things, and it's obvious why. *Your room's such a mess all the time, how do you expect to find anything in it?*"

Note if you will that throughout this book we try to kill two birds with one stone whenever possible. With practice, you'll be able to develop your own original ideas for dealing with these—and other—small problems.

Now it's time to deal with the rental of the synagogue for Bar Mitzvah morning. Fortunately, many temples subscribe to the traditional, altruistic, and *mitzvah-dicke* belief that since you pay dues each year, and since you are a good and loyal member of the congregation who can always be counted on to give generously to the building fund (including the "one time special assessment" which seems to crop up every year), you shouldn't have to pay extra for the use of the sanctuary during the big event.

Unfortunately, there seems to be a vicious, selfish, and growing trend that, member or not, the Board of Trustees has voted to impose a "one time only special event assessment of One Hundred Fifty Dollars for Bar and Bat Mitzvahs—you understand, of course, it's to defray the cost of the gifts the Sisterhood and Men's Club will give the celebrant."

Remember, the Synagogue gets a special rate for the Kiddush cup or the *Soncino* Talmud they're going to give the kid. If they're out-of-pocket fifty bucks, that's a lot. Tote it up: One Hundred Dollars clear profit. They've learned the game, even if they haven't read this book.

NOTE

This is not to say that I begrudge the Temple a thing. They do *mitzvot* by the score and I totally endorse *everything* they do. I am certain, for example, that they will stock this book in their gift shop, and what a *wonderful* thing it is for everyone concerned when you buy it. Everybody makes out, you, the Temple, even me.

Anyway, you can't really protest the fee directly. You must appeal to equity, justice and fair play. Picture a conversation similar to this one. Someone, usually the President of the congregation, has the final say, so we'll use him or her.

You: "Hello, Meyer? This is Abby. You know, Abby Adams? My eldest, David, goes to school with your daughter Phyllis? Lovely child, lovely. Children are such a blessing, aren't they? David and I are always saying what a *balabuste* she'll make? Oh? I'm sorry, I didn't know that. Left school and joined a commune, just like that? Oy! Well, as I've always said, children can really fool you sometimes. Listen, Meyer, that's not really why I called. I see that the synagogue sent me a bill for a hundred-fifty dollars for Herschel's Bar Mitzvah. Is this something new?"

PRESIDENT: "No, we've always had it. Every time there's a Bar or Bat Mitzvah."

You: "But I was billed a hundred-fifty dollars for the religious school in addition to my regular dues. That doesn't make sense."

PRESIDENT: "Yes, well, ummm…that's something the Board decided."

You: "Look, Mister President. Herschel's not even going to use the school after his Bar Mitzvah. You mean I have to pay a whole year in advance and he's not even going to use it half that time?"

PRESIDENT: "That's the way we operate, uh, Abby."

Now it's time to start hauling out the heavy artillery.

YOU: "Wait a minute. They didn't have a special Bar Mitzvah teacher for Herschel this year. He got stuck in a class with seventh graders, for God's sake! Learning about the same Abraham, Isaac and Jacob business he learned in first grade. My cousin Beryl (Yep! Same one we used for the cantor) had to teach him his whole Bar Mitzvah. The Rabbi was too busy, and your Board of Trustees didn't pay any attention when I complained."

PRESIDENT: "You complained??"

YOU: "I'm complaining right now. That's a complaint, isn't it?"

PRESIDENT: "But you said you complained to the Board of Trustees…"

YOU: "*Nu*, Meyer, you're not a trustee? I'm complaining to you. I assume it's going to get back to the Board of Trustees."

Now you've got him on the defensive. Don't lose the momentum.

YOU: "Look, Meyer, what you've got is a lousy religious school. It's fortunate that Herschel's as bright as he is, or the whole school would be embarrassed. Luckily for you, my cousin Beryl sent Herschel a tape from Congregation *Yigal ben Hamotzi* in White Plains, New York. Now there's a *real* religious school! An administrator *and a* principal *and* a curriculum director, a school counselor *and* a school psychologist. Five hundred students in that school and with good reason!" (It is critically important that you mention at least one and hopefully two or more things your religious school does *not* have. No one's going to check on a temple two thousand miles away. They wouldn't make the toll call.)

PRESIDENT: "Look, Abby (now very defensive), what would the school be like if everyone thought like you and refused to pay?"

YOU: (The *coup de grace*) *"You'd have a better school, that's what!* Look, Meyer, I'll pay one of the charges, but not the other. If you really want to be fair about this, I should only pay half of the religious school, seventy-five dollars, and after all the years I've been here, the Temple should give me the space. But I don't want to get a reputation for being tight-fisted. So I'm volunteering to pay a hundred-fifty, including the school, and that's that."

PRESIDENT: "But the Board..."

YOU: "Take that back to your Board, Meyer. Of course, if you want me to come and address the Board, I'll be happy to tell them a thing or two or three."

PRESIDENT: "No, no. I'll see what I can do. Perhaps an accommodation can be made in your case, but I wouldn't want this to get around."

YOU: "Of course not, Meyer, it's between us friends. Oh, and one thing more."

PRESIDENT: "What's that?"

YOU: "I really am sorry to hear about Paula..."

PRESIDENT: "Phyllis."

YOU: "Phyllis, I mean. It's a shame, really. By the way, David just heard from U.C. San Diego. He was accepted. It was really nice talking to you, Meyer. I'm glad to know I always have a friend at the temple I can count on."

Chances are 50-50 that's the last you'll hear of the one-time charge. The worst-case scenario is that the Treasurer will send you a bill for the next year. You have two ways of dealing with it:

1. Write a nasty note on the bill such as, "President Abramson and I discussed this some time ago. We don't pay when there's no value given." And send the bill back in the self-

addressed envelope the synagogue sends for payment. (Note: They never send a self-addressed *stamped* envelope); or

2. Ignore the bill completely. They'll keep sending it for a time—maybe even a couple of years—but what are they going to do, kick you out of the congregation if you pay your dues? Of course not.

$ 5 $

HALL RENTAL AND DECORATIONS

You really want to spend five hundred bucks on a hall? That's not only high, that's *m'shugah!* Better you should negotiate to use the synagogue hall. Even then, you insist they should throw in the tables, chairs, silverware, plates, coffee pots, etc., which they have in the back room anyway; and the janitor, who is, after all, on salary. Whatever we spend, we'll save some money on the "accoutrements," so it's not a total loss.

Decorations. Surely you weren't going to spend two-hundred-fifty dollars on decorations. A few balloons, you wrap up some old bricks in gift wrap as a centerpiece, believe me, you don't need more. You're going to have more than enough activity going on. Decorations will only detract. Since you didn't rent the Hilton Hotel, you rely on "the wonderful spirit that will infuse the celebration." Besides, too many decorations make things look artificial.

5

HALL RENTAL AND DECORATIONS

[illegible]

$ **6** $

FLOWERS

Not all Bar Mitzvahs have flowers. But the classy ones do, and let's face it, you're out to produce the biggest event the temple has ever seen. You don't want to scrimp on something like flowers.

A little research is in order. In order to conduct this investigation, you need to know a few preliminary items of importance:

1. Bar Mitzvahs take place on Saturday morning. Weddings, communions, and Christian events take place on Saturday night or Sunday. This is good if you're using this book to plan a Bar Mitzvah. Not quite so good if you're planning a Saturday evening or Sunday event.

2. Historically, in the United States there are more Christians than Jews in any given community. This means that you can count on at least one Christian event being held *somewhere* in your city, town, or *shtetl* the same weekend as Herschel's Bar Mitzvah.

3. Conservation is "in." Ecology is "in." Recycling is most certainly "in."

4. There is bound to be at least one Jewish florist in your town.

5. Alternatively, your husband, wife, or some relative is a doctor, lawyer, certified public accountant, or someone who can do a "trade-off" with the florist.

I hope by this time the picture is becoming clear.

The first thing you do is consult the "professional" (they like that phrase, even if the "C.P.A." means "cleaning, pressing and alterations") and convince him (or her in this politically correct era) that he'd be doing a real *mitzvah,* and it wouldn't take very much of his (her) time to write a will, prepare a simple tax return, or remove a wart from the florist's sister's face in exchange for flowers.

This being done, you exercise just slightly more *chutzpah.* You ask the relative to call a florist he (or she) knows and make the arrangements for you. Usually this is no big deal. If it is, you remind your uncle-the-lawyer that if he does something "free" for the florist, it's good advertising. Florists have friends who get hit by cars too, and he never can tell…the florist may send him some "real" business.

One last thing. You tell your uncle you want to write the Bar Mitzvah off on your tax return as "entertainment expense" (ha! ha!), so you'd appreciate if he could get a "paid" invoice from the florist in a reasonable amount, say two hundred dollars.

O.K. The first half is over. Now it's time for the real action—your first profit.

You call various churches and see what events they have coming up the weekend of January 15. You probably won't have to look too far. Chances are you won't even have to make a toll call.

Then, in your best ecumenical manner, you ask to speak to the Pastor, Priest, or whoever's in charge. Here you play it "white bread-and-mayonnaise" all the way.

PASTOR: "Pastor Martin here."

YOU: "Reverend Doctor Martin? This is Mrs. Goldfarb-Adams. I'm not one of your parishioners. In fact I'm a member of the Hebrew faith, and I was wondering if you might please give me some help?"

PASTOR: "Whatever I can do, Mrs. Goldbarth, uh, Adams?"

YOU: "That's correct. My, you *do* have a way with names Reverend Martin. Anyway, I was thinking about how ecumenical

we've all become. (Good buzz word. Christians like to use it.) One big, happy family under God."

PASTOR: (Beaming) "Of course, Mrs....?"

You: "Why not call me 'Abigail' if you will, Father? That's my *Christian* name."

PASTOR: "And a fine Biblical name it is, Abigail. Now then, you spoke about my helping you?"

You: "Yes, Father. You know, we all share a need to preserve our planet. This is an effort in which we're joined in brotherhood."

PASTOR: (Chuckling) "And sisterhood, too. (Heavy-handed humor is not limited to Cantors). My little idea of a joke, Abigail."

You: "Anyway, Pastor, my son Herschel is having his Bar Mitzvah on January fifteenth..."

PASTOR: "Oh, yes, the Jewish confirmation. Lovely event, lovely. My congratulations to you. I believe they say '*Mazel Tov?*'"

You: "How clever you are, Reverend Martin! As I was saying, I noticed you'll be marrying Christine Perkins and Wesley Bradford the following day. We've commissioned some lovely floral arrangements from Sebastian Pincus—he's truly an artist in floral sculpture, you've undoubtedly seen his work—and I was thinking perhaps the Perkinses and we could make double use of the flowers and share the expense. Sort of make it a truly joint Judaeo-Christian (another good buzz word) undertaking and contribute our small part to conservation and recycling at the same time."

PASTOR: "That's a wonderful idea, Abigail. How absolutely thoughtful of you. I'm overwhelmed. Tell you what. I'll telephone Mrs. Perkins for you right now. Better yet, she comes to Bible study class every Wednesday night. I'll mention it to her in front of the entire group. This could really start something wonderful between our congregations."

You: "Oh, father. I'm so impressed by your brilliance. I wouldn't dream of taking credit for an idea of this magnitude. It's *your* contribution to the betterment of Judaeo-Christian understanding. Are you sure you won't let me call Mrs. Perkins?"

PASTOR: "No, my good woman, I insist that I make the contact myself."

And so forth.

$ 7 $

VIDEOTAPING
THE BAR MITZVAH

In the past several years, our civilization has seen a technological explosion to rival that of the Renaissance: computers, FAX machines, satellite communications, the VCR and the Camcorder. With the development of these toys has come the Videotape Revolution.

Nowadays, everything is recorded for posterity: births, operations, deaths, little Susie losing her first tooth. Why should the Bar Mitzvah be an exception? Let's face it, it's the last event where you'll be able to record Herschel without, "Aww, ma, it's so embarrassing! Besides, I've got a date."

Combined with the televideo revolution comes an even better development as far as you're concerned. Look through any university catalogue. You'll see "TCF"—telecommunications and film—as a major. Attend any class in that department—assuming it's not impacted (totally sold out)—and you'll see the room packed with budding writers, directors and cinematographers, each of whom is going to make a million dollars some time during his first five years out of school. Sure. But only if daddy has invested ten million in a trust fund for him, or if he hits the lottery.

But hope springs eternal. Every generation looks for "the man with the big cigar" who is going to discover this hero of heroes. Who knows what event will trigger lady fortune? Richard Dreyfuss scored in "The Apprenticeship of Duddy Kravitz," a Canadian low-budget flick some years back. Oddly enough, young Duddy was "discovered" when he filmed a Bar Mitzvah.

Your approach is direct. No need for subterfuge. You go to the nearest college or university and seek an audience with the Chairman of the Telecommunications Department, or, even better, you latch on to the graduate T.A. (teacher's assistant) who's making minimum wage lecturing to bored undergrads in Cinematography 101. Never mind that what most of these students have on their mind during lectures is boffing the blonde bombshell in the second row while a buddy shoots porn movies of the grand event. We're talking business here.

The device is simple. You enter into a straight business deal with the T.A. He gives an "extra credit" assignment: a maximum of three undergrads can sign up for "On-the-job-training lab." That means shooting the Herschel Adams Bar Mitzvah. You sweeten the deal considerably by entering into an arrangement where, after you get the first three copies of the video free, you and the T.A. split profits on any videos sold at the Bar Mitzvah. At ten dollars a pop, you suggest that the T.A. might make more in a morning than he would in a month at the college. It's not really fraud as long as you don't mention numbers. He'll be lucky if he makes two sales. I mean, would you be interested in buying a videotape of another kid's Bar Mitzvah? Only if you're the type who loves an evening of suffering through someone else's home movies.

Most likely, the Teacher's Assistant will want to do the video himself because otherwise he might have to split the profits with one of the undergrads. To top things off, he'll probably bring the blonde bombshell in the second row to the Bar Mitzvah and he wouldn't want any undergrad horning (or horny-ing) in on his time.

This is yet another example of the famed adage: Old age and treachery will defeat youth and vigor every time!

$ 8 $
THE MUSIC AND ENTERTAINMENT

O.K., folks, *IT'S SHOW TIME!* There's no business like show business! In short, P.T. Barnum's old saw, "There's a sucker born every minute," applies to entertainers—particularly *young* entertainers—in spades!

If you think the cantor is shooting for the Metropolitan Opera and the cinematographer is gunning for Hollywood, you ain't seen nothing 'til you've seen "The Band."·

If you made your own son stick with piano or guitar lessons long enough, you've been through the experience. Four kids get together in a garage. (Remember the old VM phonographs that always gave you an electric shock when you threw a dance or party in the garage? Modern electronics aren't much different.) A drummer, two guitars and an electric bass, all fighting to prove they can be heard on the other side of the planet. One of the guitarists is a "vocalist." Never mind the "singer" stuff, this here's a "superstar on vocals." He can imitate any "KISS," "Guns 'n' Roses," or "Pearl Jam" megahit of the last ten years. (This assumes you're "hip" and have heard of any of these musical legends-in-their-own-minds.) They rehearse all night, or at least until some neighbor, who can't stand hearing the same series of four notes played at ear-busting zillion-decibel volume, calls

**P.T. Barnum's old saw,
"There's a sucker born every minute,"
applies to young entertainers in spades.**

the parent-in-charge or the police (who always take three hours to come and break it up).

Unfortunately for them—very fortunately for you—the vast majority of these waiting-to-be-discovered headliners have no showcase for their talent other than the garage. The "man with the big cigar" is not known to frequent such places. And the star-studded career the band anticipates is stillborn.

You, too, can be a heroine! A knightess in shining armor! A talent scout! You offer to provide the band a forum, an audience, a launching pad from which they can soar to the stars. And, to boot, they only have to pay *you* twenty-five dollars "to help defray expenses."

The rules change if you're dealing with a band that has any Jewish members. They're usually on the same wavelength as you. They know they're only using this "band" *shtick* to put them through university so they can become doctors, lawyers, CPAs, or "Jewish engineers" (translation: businessmen), and get to the real bucks. Never mind the "experience," they're looking for *gelt.*

I've heard it said that one's strongest point is also his greatest weakness. If money is the prime motivator, then money it shall be—provided it's not *your* cash outlay.

Whether you're dealing with a Jewish or non-Jewish band, the problem is only a matter of degree. If you feel in a particularly generous mood, you suggest that a non-Jewish band might put a basket in front of the bandstand and you'll pay them forty percent of what guests drop in the basket. A Jewish bandleader (and of course the Jew will be the band *leader*) will insist on seventy-five percent of the take. Yield to such blackmail if you must, but *never under any circumstances* give the band a guaranteed minimum. If the man with the big cigar isn't willing to gamble on them, why should you?

Now that monetary considerations have been taken care of, the second—and far more important—problem rears its ugly head. An established, professional Jewish band—"Meyer Mereminsky and his Merry Minskys—Better than a night at the Follies" (Heavy-handed humor abounds in every field of endeavor!)—has played every big Bar Mitzvah in the last twenty-five years. They play all the *frailach's*, *k'satzkes*, and *horas*. And you can dance to everything they play. They're good, damn good. And they cost Twenty-Five Hundred Dollars a pop, none of this nickel-and-dime *chazzerai*.

O.K., you've gotten a free band, but if they stick to their repertoire, which consists entirely of "Sanitarium," "Crazy Babies," "Pain Riot" and "Highway to Hell," (I've never heard of them either, I got the titles from my own teenagers) you're going to have a fairly empty dance floor not to mention a lawsuit or two from hearing loss. To make matters worse, they believe what they play is music, and everything else is "from the stone age."

Is the problem insurmountable? Only if "Guns and Gefilte Fish," or whatever they call themselves can't read music. That may cut out ninety percent of "bands" right there.

Assume, however, that the "musicians" have at least a Neanderthal's ability to follow notes. Now it's time to find someone who can give the band a "long, serious talk." That "someone" should be anyone who's had sufficient experience with *real* music and knows the ins-and-outs of the business. If there's a local boy who made good as a football or baseball player (at least Triple-A leagues), that's sufficient credentials. If you can't find one, there are others who might make a good substitute:

1. The blonde bombshell from the "Videotape" section above.
2. Anyone who's ever had anything to do with a record, a movie or a TV show, even if it only amounted to sending in a script which got a polite rejection notice.
3. Someone who's recently appeared in a play at the local college.

4. Someone who's "managed" a band. Preferably someone who
   smokes a big cigar.

This resident *maven* (expert), must impart the following message
to the band, and this message must somehow stick: "You are never
going to get anywhere unless you are *different* from the other five
thousand bands in the area. In order to be different, you must have a
gimmick. A gimmick is something *original*, something that no one else
does. (This is circuitous reasoning, but even music-brains "dig" it.)
Such a gimmick is *not* dressing in four different outfits and smelling
like the underside of a toilet at a rest stop off Interstate Ten. Here's an
idea for a gimmick—the kind of music no other band plays! Take my
word for it, it works! You'll be invited to play at other events. For
money! And you'll get a name!"

By this time, you hope the band will be all ears—or at least that
part of their ears that can still hear.

MAVEN: "Why not try to play real *Jewish* music?"
BANDLEADER: "What? You've got to be kidding. That stuff is so far
out that it was never even 'in.'"
MAVEN: "Ever heard of *Fiddler on the Roof?*"
BANDLEADER: "Is that a local group?"
MAVEN: "Yeah. Local as in world tour."
BANDLEADER: "You mean like Springsteen?"
MAVEN: "You got it! Hey! You're really pretty bright after all!"
BANDLEADER: "How come I've never heard of this 'Fiddler' group
if they're so hot?"
MAVEN: "A bit before your time, I'm afraid."
BANDLEADER: "That's what I told you. Years before my time."
MAVEN: "Sure! Just like The Beatles or the Stones. Fifties and
sixties are *in*—maybe you're not with the program." (Again, find a
current put-down statement and use it. That language hits home.
Even the bandleader 'digs' it.)

BANDLEADER: (A little bit interested at last) "Well, let's just say I'd be willing to consider what you have to say. Now my group's really a bunch of great musicians, but this Jewish music stuff is a little strange, flutes and bagpipes and probably weird chords that nobody's ever heard of."

MAVEN: (Coup de grace time!) "That's just it! The reason nobody's doing it is because they think it's too hard. It isn't. It's done in a minor key, but it usually uses only three different chords, and the rhythm's a piece of cake."

BANDLEADER: "Yeah, but? (Quiet embarrassment) Uh…it's not me, of course, I know exactly what you mean, but some of my guys…that is…they've never learned to read music…"

MAVEN: "No problem! Just play chords—D minor, G minor, A-seven. And start clapping. The people know the words and they'll be clapping and dancing and making so much noise all you have to do is invent as you go along."

BANDLEADER: "Yeah? Then why haven't I ever heard of this stuff?"

MAVEN: "Because what goes around comes around. Reggae was 'in' in the fifties and 'out' 'til the nineties. Something called *klezmer* music's the hottest thing in New York right now. Where did it start? Poland, a hundred years ago. And what was the biggest album of the nineties? The Beatles Anthology album—recycled sixties music. Like you said about Springsteen—he goes on world tour with it. And there just aren't enough groups to fill the gap. Let's face it, you aren't gonna' be competing with eight zillion other groups. You can still do your own thing—but now you've got a little extra 'insurance.' The Adams family's well known in this town. They could have chosen any band they wanted for this event. But they saw something in you—originality, foresight, a band that's *going places!*" (Do not, of course, use words like "musicianship" or "intelligence." This book refuses to encourage outright lies.)

Actually, you can stay "One step ahead of the Joneses"—or the Cohens or whoever—and still save money! Do the same thing with *another* band! Only this time the maven should encourage a different gimmick—let's say waltzes or polkas or even 1950's-era early rock-n' roll. The specialties are limitless.

Now for the final master stroke. Nowadays, for whatever reason, the "Disk Jockey" is the big thing. This is an ersatz "personality"—someone who brings "star" quality to the Bar Mitzvah.

For your purposes, the "Disk Jockey" might mean an expenditure of a few bucks, but what it really means is that you have a safety valve. Someone who'll play pre-recorded *music*—just in case the band(s) turn out to be as awful as you think they'll be.

In every city or town of any size, at least one hundred percent of children above the age of six listen to a "Top Forty" station. There are usually more of these stations around than there are listeners and you wouldn't be caught dead listening to any of them, but that's not your concern at the moment. We're talking saving money here.

Kids who listen to the *dreck* (excrement) these stations play go nuts over "DJ's." As part of your research, listen to a couple of these stations for about ten minutes, even if you can't stand it. But listen to these stations only on weekends. Saturday afternoon, Sunday morning or Sunday night are "prime times." For these are the times when the "regulars"—the full-time, legitimate air personalities—take time off to be with their families and give their brains a chance to mend by listening to Vivaldi.

You'll probably notice right off the bat that the male voices on the weekend shifts sound a little higher-pitched than usual, and the female voices tend to intersperse their comments with "uh…uh… that's a really heavy tune…" (or some equally inane bit of "wisdom.") There's a reason for that. The part-timers are usually awestruck high school kids, who think being on the radio is the beginning of their rocket to stardom. Long ago, station managers learned that they could get these would-be celebrities for minimum wage and that shameless profiteering continues to this day. Good for them. Great for you!

Two ways of doing it here. Telephone call or letter. The latter's much better. The "air personality" sees his or her name in print—and it "really impresses the boss 'cause it's fan mail." The kid's real name is Irving Kachinsky, but he never uses it on the air. It's "Irv Kay" or some such. Anyway, make sure you mark the letter "Personal and Confidential"—this makes for real interest:

Mr. Irv Kay
K-102 Radio—The Big Boss
Henryville, IL

PERSONAL AND CONFIDENTIAL

Dear Mr. Kay:

I must begin by saying I don't usually listen to Top Forty music, and I hardly ever listen to K-102. However in the last several weeks my teenage daughter, who's 5'1" tall, dark haired and goes to Henryville High (substitute the words "son, who's 6' tall, dark-haired and plays football for Henryville High" if you're writing to a female DJ), and her friends have constantly told me, "Mom, you've just got to listen to Irv Kay, the weekend man (never use anything but 'man'—that carries a tone of authority) on The Big Boss, K-102."

Finally, just to get them off my back, I turned the station on, and I was surprised to hear someone who not only played their kind of music—which I still don't like—but who sounded like a real professional (that's the key word in the business, the hook on which they'll bite every time)—someone with a rich, dynamic voice who knew what he was doing every step of the way—a real air personality (another wonderful buzz word).

Mr. Kay, my son Herschel is having a Bar Mitzvah on January 15. It's a major event, and I'm sure someone of your intelligence is aware of just how important a Bar Mitzvah is! We'll be having over a hundred people of all ages—at least twenty of whom are Irv Kay fans! Teenagers of both sexes.

We need a real celebrity to help make our event a winner. While we're sure someone as well-known and popular as you doesn't really need the exposure (like hell he doesn't!), we'd feel honored if you'd consider giving us a couple of hours of your time on that afternoon. We don't ask that you do this for nothing. We're willing to pay you Ten Dollars (this is probably twice what he makes at the station) an hour plus lunch, and we'll furnish some tapes, records and equipment for you to use.

We were originally going to use Jeff Powers (this calls for research; find out from your kids who's really the most popular professional Disk Jockey in town on the biggest station and use his name) but my daughter (son) insisted that I had to use Irv Kay or no one. And, after I listened to you, I found out she was right!

Could you please drop me a line at [your address] or call me at [your phone number] as soon as possible so we can finalize arrangements.

Respectfully,
(*Oy!* Does this get to them every time!)

Mrs. Abigail Adams.

cc: Station Manager, K-102

Of course you may want to use your own variation on the theme. But again, you get the picture. You've got the band—hopefully even two of them—and you've got the "air personality" for insurance, "just in case."

And just think of the tongues that'll click after the Bar Mitzvah. "You should have been at the Adams Bar Mitzvah! *Two* bands *and* a Disk Jockey! They must have *poured* money into that event!"

$ 9 $

THE PROGRAMS

So far I've been talking about conserving money. Not bad, but, to be perfectly frank, that's of secondary interest. Now comes the really important part of the book. This is where you *make money!* (That got your interest pretty fast!)

At every Bar Mitzvah you walk into the foyer of the Synagogue and an usher—usually a kid brother or one of the temple "elders"—hands you an eight by eleven inch piece of paper, folded once to make four "pages." If you've been to a Bar Mitzvah, you know what I mean. They all look the same. The front page may have a photocopy of the kid's certificate showing that he became Bar Mitzvah on such-and-such a date. Maybe there's a bit of amateur calligraphy saying gushy stuff like "In Honor of Our Son's Entry into the Covenant with G-d." (Don't forget, the real entry into the Covenant was when the kid was eight days old and had a quarter of his *schmeckele* cut off.)

Inside, usually on the second page, is the name of various relatives or friends called to the *Bimah* to recite blessings or walk around the room holding the Torah scroll. That's usually followed by a poor woodcut which usually has no meaning except it's somehow supposed to convey that the celebrant is entering into something at least as old as the woodcut. The third and fourth pages usually contain the printed Hebrew Torah portion and the *Haftarah*, accompanied by a translation into old-fashioned English. At the end, there's usually another little woodcut—what they used to call a "filler" in newspapers. That's it. Period. Dull. Boring. And most important, the complete failure of something that could have been a spectacular income generator!

All right, folks, now comes the key to the castle, the idea which will be worth far more than you paid for this book, and I'm not even asking for a percentage: *ADVERTISING*.

And, best of all, you don't even sully your own character by having to solicit the ads!

How many times have you been hounded by young kids—let's face it, by obnoxious teen-aged kids as well—selling you something. Cakes and cookies outside the supermarket to pay for their trip to Peoria. Girl scout cookies. Subscriptions to magazines so that the seller can win a genuine, superfabulous five-speed calculator with a retail value of $59.95 (which was made in Indonesia for $1.25). Candies imprinted with the name of the Hoboken Hospital for Homeless Hoboes. You name it, there's always a reason, and kids tug at your heartstrings and your purse-strings, if for no other reason than you want to get them off your back!

This time, however, the kids are selling something different, something truly worthwhile! And you give them ten percent of everything they sell.

Before you send them out, however, you do some intelligent planning.

1. You need a theme for the sale. You can't simply imply that it's going to benefit a specific person. No indeed. It has to be much more generic. It's Herschel's Bar Mitzvah. The kid will be thirteen. He's not a sweet little angel anymore, and he certainly is *not* a "man" (his speech notwithstanding). You don't want to refer to him as a teenager, because that has bad connotations for everyone in the world except teenagers and their adoring younger siblings. Herschel is now a *Youth*—and everyone wants to help *Youth*. It is *Youth* who

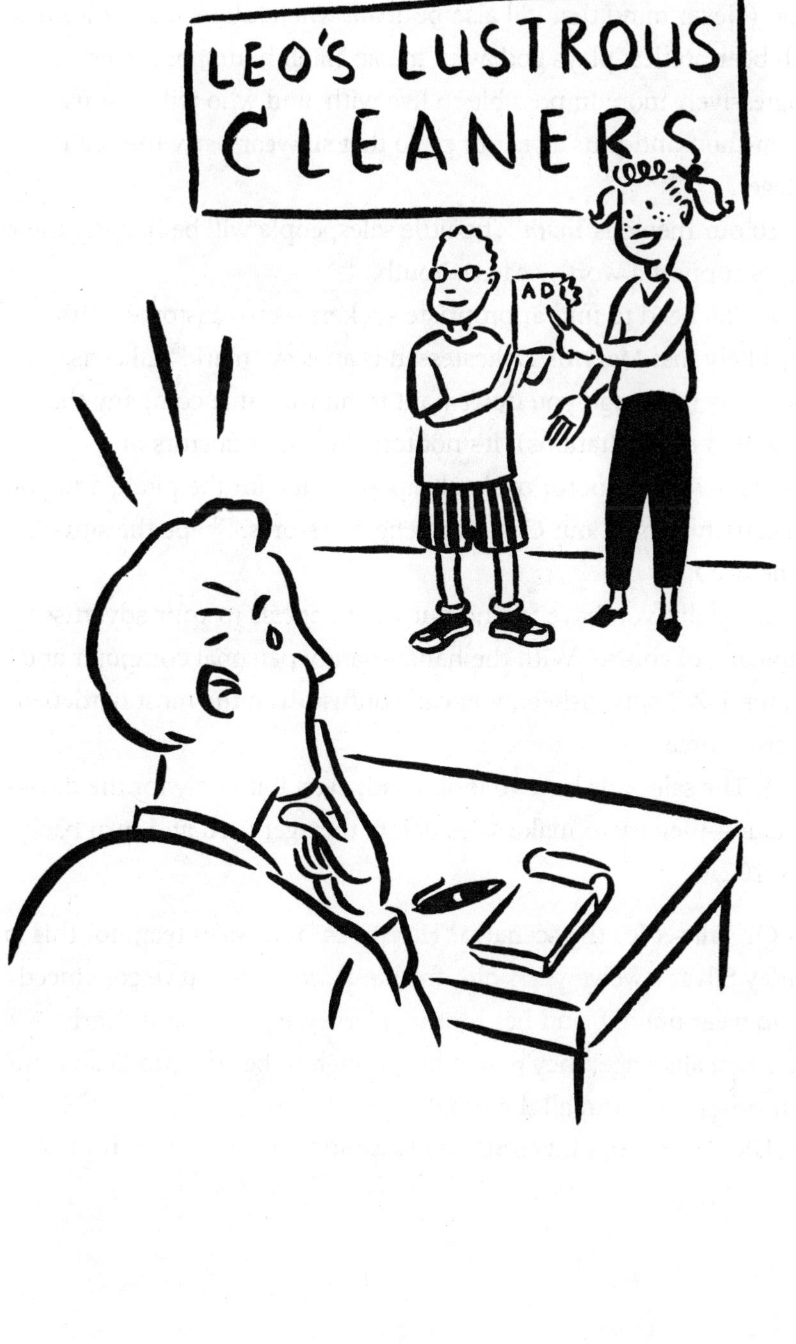
LEO'S LUSTROUS CLEANERS
AD

win scholarships, *Youth* who will be our future leaders, *Youth* who will make the grand discoveries that whirl us to the planets and back. (Never mind that it'll also be *Youth* who clutters up our homes with beer bottles, plays godawful music 'til all hours, becomes progressively more impossible to live with, and who will cost us fifteen-thousand-plus a year to go to that six-year party they call college).

So our theme is *Youth*. The little salespeople will be helping their targets support a worthy cause: Youth.

2. You need to find appropriate suckers—er—customers. It's very likely that Marvin's Delicatessen is an easy "mark." Likewise Coca Cola (although you don't want to hit the same company that sponsored the invitations). It's not too likely that doctors or lawyers—who are notoriously cheap—will fall for the pitch, and you can certainly count out Christian religious stores. Shape the situation to the need.

3. Finally, you have to find out what appeals to your advertiser. Numbers, of course. With the handy-dandy personal computer and a Lotus 1-2-3 spreadsheet, you can confuse even the most hardened, resistive force.

4. The saleskids have to look good, even if it's only for the day— or hour—they try to make sales before they get tired and turn back to K-102.

OK, all set for the scenario? Here goes. Your sales team for this is Shirley Silver (twelve years old, freckle-faced, and you've convinced her to wear braids), and her brother Harvey, eight (a particularly cute, appealing age; they're just big enough to be still-cuddleable and their noses don't run all the time).

The scene: Leo's Lustrous Dry Cleaning. Owner: Leo Schwartz.

SHIRLEY: "Hi, Mr. Schwartz. Remember me? I'm Shirley Silver. My dad comes in all the time. He brings his shirts in to be laundered every week."

OWNER: "Sure, Shirley, of course I do. My, how you've grown. (This is an abject lie. He doesn't recall ever seeing the kid, but she's so friendly and charming he can never admit it. Besides, who knows? Her father really may be a customer). How can I help you, honey?"

SHIRLEY: "Well, sir, I'm trying to save money to go to Youth State—you know, the big nationwide event that's being held in Chicago next year—young people from forty-five states will be there. And I'm selling..."

OWNER: (His eyes start to roll up into his head) "I'm not really interested in buying..."

HARVEY: "Oh, it's not buying anything, Mister Leo. It's something to benefit *Youth*." (Good delivery, kid! Perfect! Use of his first name to build familiarity, and use of a big word, "benefit," which indicates the little guy's as intelligent as he looks!)

OWNER: "Oh?"

SHIRLEY: (Stepping right back in) "Yes, Mister Schwartz. This is not like girl scout cookies or a bake sale. This is something where everyone wins. You help Youth and you'll probably make money from it."

OWNER (a little suspicious): "What do you mean?"

SHIRLEY: Herschel Adams is having his Bar Mitzvah on January fifteenth. (She pulls out an eight by eleven inch mock-up of a slick, four-color imprint which reads:

HERSCHEL SCHMENDRICK GOLDFARB-ADAMS
COMMEMORATIVE BAR MITZVAH PROGRAM
and
PREFERRED MERCHANTS
BUSINESS DIRECTORY
to the
City of Henryville
SPECIAL EDITION

*"All you need to know
about the finest places to go!"*

OWNER: "What's this??? Bar Mitzvah program and preferred business directory??? (By this time, he's thunderstruck by the *chutzpah* of this idea more than anything else.) You're joking!"

HARVEY: "No, sir. It's a really good idea. And I think it would really help your business, Mister Leo." (Another prepared script. Out of the mouth of babes, and all that.)

SHIRLEY: "Seriously, Mister Schwartz, you'll have to admit it's an original idea."

OWNER: "My God, it's…it's…can they do that kind of thing at a Bar Mitzvah?"

SHIRLEY: "Perfectly legal, Mister Schwartz. Strictly Kosher, as a matter of fact. They do it at the Synagogue all the time. Why, they take ads for their bid-and-buy auction, the 25th Anniversary of the Building Fund Party, the Chanukah Dance…"

OWNER: (Recovering a bit). "Wait a minute, here. You said it benefits *Youth.*"

SHIRLEY: "Well, Herschel's a youth. I'm a youth. Little Harvey here's a youth. And you certainly want to benefit *Jewish* youth, don't you, Mister Schwartz? I mean, over at the high school Saint Mary's

Church gives a scholarship each year, the First Assembly of God gives a scholarship, the Women's Christian Temperance Union..." (Go on, girl! Learn how to give out good old Jewish guilt early in life. It's good practice for later!)

OWNER: "Yes, but this isn't a scholarship, it's a...a..."

SHIRLEY: "It's a real *Mitzvah,* is that what you're trying to say, Mister Schwartz? Now remember, I said it benefits all of us, you included?"

OWNER: "Me?"

SHIRLEY: "Of course, Mr. Schwartz. There'll be over a hundred people at the Adams Bar Mitzvah. They'll all see the program, and they'll take it home to their families to see all of the nifty ads inside."

OWNER: "Wait a minute! I've been to Bar Mitzvahs before. You get a piece of white paper folder into quarters and you throw it away or your kids make paper airplanes out of it right after the event."

SHIRLEY: "Yes, sir, that's the ordinary flyer they give out. But the Adams Bar Mitzvah will be different. They're going to have smooth paper, like they have in the magazines, and a heavy-duty permanent plastic cover. We've got over a hundred ads already. (Well...that may be stretching it a little, but who knows? By the time all the ads are sold there may be five hundred.) And we're limiting it to one ad per business. Ten of us kids are out selling the ads. Judy Sherman's supposed to see Mr. Goldblum at Golden Glow Cleaners this afternoon but if I can sign you up first, that's just tough for her."

OWNER: (Scowling) "Goldblum? The *shmatte* cleaner? You know, he dilutes his cleaning solvent with water, cheap b—"

HARVEY: "My dad says you're the very best Mister Leo. That's why we want the honor of signing you up."

SHIRLEY: "Shush, Harvey! We don't want to force anyone to do anything. Why don't you think about it, Mister Schwartz? I'd like to leave you a computer print-out that Mister Adams did that shows how telephone advertising works."

OWNER: "Telephone advertising? This isn't the yellow pages."

SHIRLEY: "Of course it isn't, Mister Schwartz. But it could become like a *neighborhood* yellow pages. You know, the Yellow Pages is such a big, heavy book, and if people want to know what's right in the neighborhood, why should they pull out such a big old thing? But you just think about it, and I'll be back another time."

OWNER: "But Goldblum? You said the other girl's gonna' see him this afternoon."

SHIRLEY: "Oh, I'm sure she won't make the sale that fast either. (Smiling her sweetest smile.) But it is first-come, first-served, and my dad and I would feel so bad if he got into the directory and you didn't."

OWNER: "How much is it?"

SHIRLEY: (Brightening) "Only a hundred dollars a page…"

OWNER: (Exploding) "*A hundred dollars!*…Did you say a hundred dollars???"

SHIRLEY: "That's for the whole page, Mister Schwartz. Hardly anyone except Coca Cola and American Airlines are taking out that kind of ad."

OWNER: "Did you say Coca-Cola?"

SHIRLEY: "Oh, sure. Youth, and all. You know. They spend money on anything having to do with kids. Now I was thinking more of a quarter page for you."

OWNER: "A quarter page?"

SHIRLEY: "Sure. It's only thirty dollars. And it's not just typed in. You get to put in your own card, or you can print greetings from your whole family, whatever else you want."

OWNER: "Thirty dollars isn't so bad. How much does half a page run?"

SHIRLEY: "Sixty."

OWNER: "Could you make it fifty-five?"

SHIRLEY: (Aha! The businessman wants to make a deal. Don't press your luck, kid. Mrs. Adams said start at sixty, go down to fifty if you have to. At fifty-five bucks that means five dollars fifty cents for ten minutes worth of work. There's not that much difference between five-fifty and six. Besides, with these stupid pigtails Shirley can still get into the afternoon movie for 12-and-under and have two-fifty left over). "Well…I think Mrs. Adams would let me do that. Tell you what. You sign up right now and if you can pay me in advance, I'll make sure she does. I'll telephone Judy Sherman at lunch and tell her not to bother with Mister Goldblum. Besides, my dad went there once when you were on vacation and he said he'd never go back there again."

End of scene. End of sale.

Of course, not all of them will be so easy. But let's say you get twenty-five pages of ads. Five full page ads (banks, savings and loans who want to show they're not broke, maybe even Coca-Cola), another eight pages of half-page ads (real estate brokers and insurance brokers, you don't give the one-of-a-kind-only pitch to them), ten pages of quarter page ads (this time Shirley caught Leo for the half-page, but most businessmen will stay with the quarter page), and another two pages of "Greetings"—one-eighth of a page at fifteen dollars a pop.

Let's stop writing a minute to tote up the score:

Five pages, $100 per page	$ 500
Eight pages of half pages at $110 per page	880
Ten pages of quarter page ads, $120 per page	1,200
Two pages of greetings, $120 per page	240
Inside front cover	150
Inside back cover	150
Total advertising:	**$ 3,120**
Less sales commission to the kids (10%)	(312)
Net profit from sales:	**$ 2,808**

I know of some people who try to get away with *spending* that on a Bar Mitzvah, and that's for the cheapest kind of all, with less than fifty people!

You are now using *sechel* (common sense), and that translates into not only surviving the Bar Mitzvah but making a *profit* from it as well.

I'm sure you've got your own ideas forming by now. But it's like anything else: Plan your work and work your plan, and you're sure to succeed. May you have fifty pages of sales, even, God willing, a hundred twenty!

Of course, there's the expense of printing these little directories up. You've committed to a slick magazine approach. If you come in with anything less than first class, you're going to look like a *schnorrer.* Besides, better know that the Leo Schwartzes of the world are going to want a copy—and if they're done right, they're going to want several copies. Are you starting to get the picture?

Next stop, the printer.

You: "Hi, I'm Abby Adams, remember me? (Of course he doesn't, but he won't admit it). American Association of University Women, Junior League…you did the printing for us last year." (Of course, before you went, you called up someone who is a member of one of those organizations and found out who printed their program six months ago.)

Printer: "Yes, as a matter of fact, I did print up the Junior League program. Did you like it?" (Beaming with pride).

You: "Fabulous, fabulous! I keep a copy at home on my living room table, and it never fails to get compliments."

Printer: (Already entranced) "What can I do for you Mrs. Adams?"

You: "Why not call me Abby? Sort of like Abigail Adams. Her husband was a friend of Benjamin Franklin and I understand he was a printer, so maybe this generation of Adams can be friends with a printer, too." (Careful, girl. The humor's getting a little too heavy-handed even for this guy).

PRINTER: "Oh, uh, yes…Abby, then. What can I do for you?"

YOU: "I'm having a private event. My son's Bar Mitzvah. We're having about a hundred folks, just a little private party, but we've sold some advertising, so we'll need about a thirty-five page program. We'd like it done up special, plastic cover and all. But we really can't afford all that much."

PRINTER: "Hmm? Well, slick paper and all, you're looking at about two bucks a copy. How many copies do you need?"

YOU: (Looking very dejected) "About five hundred. You see, it's not only going to be a program. It's going to be a business directory. This is what I had in mind…(Show him the same mock-up that little Shirley showed the Dry Cleaner). You see, I thought we'd distribute it around town."

PRINTER: "Around town, eh? Well, we might be able to do it a little cheaper if we went photo offset and used a lighter weight paper?"

YOU: "Gosh, I don't know, Mister…?"

PRINTER: "As a matter of fact the name's Ben, but it's not Franklin." (Is there anyone in the world that doesn't have his own brand of heavy-handed humor?)

YOU: "How utterly charming! Ben the Printer. Look, I don't mind if you used a lighter grade paper, but the cover's got to be something that lasts."

PRINTER: (Taking out his pencil). "We might be able to squeak by at a dollar-fifty a copy. Seven hundred fifty bucks all told."

YOU: "Still a bit more than my husband and I thought about. I've got an idea, though. We haven't sold the back cover yet. That's the premier position. We thought we'd try for five hundred dollars for it."

PRINTER: "That's a lot of money. You might be able to get two hundred tops."

YOU: (Brightening, as if an idea just struck you between the eyes) "Listen, Ben, suppose you deduct two hundred from the seven-fifty. That'll be five-fifty and I know it's almost all profit for you."

PRINTER: "Nawww. I don't do that kind of advertising. I could knock a hundred-fifty off and bring it down to an even six hundred."

YOU: (Thinking). "Still won't work, Ben. But I could probably do it if you'd throw in a couple of hundred printed matchbooks and the same number of napkins. Real simple stuff, 'Herschel Adams' Bar Mitzvah'—just one line, any kind of type you like."

PRINTER: "Hey, I don't run a bargain basement print shop. This is first quality stuff."

YOU: (Sweetly) "I know. With your ad going on the back cover, it wouldn't be anything but first class."

PRINTER: (Resigned) "Six hundred then, cash in advance?"

YOU: "Of course. I wouldn't do it any other way."

Now let's see where you are:

1. At six hundred dollars, the cost to you is $1.20 a copy. Keep that figure in mind, because here's where you make some major league profit.

2. But it's actually less than $1.20 a copy, because you've managed to get the napkins and matchbooks thrown in. Not everyone has these things at a Bar Mitzvah, but they add class.

3. At this point, you have *two* bands, a disk jockey, printed napkins, printed matchbooks, and a program no one's going to believe.

What's more, it gets better from here!

You have printed five hundred copies of "Herschel Goldfarb-Adams Commemorative Bar Mitzvah Program *and Preferred Merchants Business Directory*" at a total cost of six hundred dollars.

Now comes the time for action. In a corporation, there are two classes of stock, "Common" and "Preferred." Hardly anyone who's not a corporate executive, a stockbroker or a lawyer knows the difference, and most people would be stunned to know that generally "Common" stock is the better of the two since it's the only one that shares in increased equity. For your purposes, you're going to go with what most people think is the difference between "Common" and "Preferred"—that is to say, if it's "Preferred" it's got to be better.

You're going to have two classes of programs for Herschel's Bar Mitzvah, just like the Opera or the Theater. The "common" is going to be the one that's handed out for free.

But you're not going to make it your usual four page—with woodcut—foldover. Oh, no. This is going to be a straight one-page job, printed on an old mimeograph machine (if you can still find them), otherwise on an old portable typewriter and photocopied on an old-fashioned copier that uses that strange-feeling paper that smells of ink-and-oil, and the ink rubs off on your hands. This is the "common" program. It'll have a brief title, "Herschel Adams Bar Mitzvah—Common Program," the names of the people involved, and that's it. No Hebrew writing, no explanation of anything. Nothing.

But for a scant five dollars more, with all proceeds going to Youth, the guests (or anyone else who wants to for that matter) can go home with the

DELUXE PREFERRED

Herschel Schmendrick Goldfarb-Adams Commemorative Bar Mitzvah Program

and

PREFERRED MERCHANTS
BUSINESS DIRECTORY
to the
CITY OF HENRYVILLE
◆ SPECIAL EDITION ◆

*"All you need to know
about the finest places to go!"*

~

Special Deluxe Souvenir Edition
Personally Autographed
by the Bar Mitzvah

**With Biographies of All Important Participants,
the Liturgy (In English and Hebrew)
And a
Description of the Significance of the Event,
Including Historic Woodcuts**

Assume you'll be able to peddle about sixty of these, maybe a hundred if you're lucky, but count on sixty. That leaves you with four hundred forty programs left to sell. Fifteen of them (at least) go out to *mishpoche* (relatives). That leaves four hundred twenty-five. You give a hundred of them to the advertisers to show that you've got class and good faith. Three-and-a-quarter to go.

You offer to let your advertisers have them at half price, two-fifty apiece. They'll be gone so fast it'll make your head spin.

Here's the tote board:

Sixty at full price	$ 300
325 at $2.50 apiece	812.50
Gross sales price	1,112.50
Less printing costs	(600.00)
Net profit	**$ 512.50**

There may be reorders from the merchants. The second printing is always cheaper than the first because the plates are already set up. At two dollars fifty cents per program, you make a clear one dollar and thirty cents per copy. The gift that keeps on giving.

$ **10** $

THE PHOTOGRAPHER

This is usually a big problem if you go to a professional. They charge and they charge—boy, do they ever!—and you'll be lucky to get out with spending under a thousand dollars. And usually what you get is a bunch of stilted-looking people, looking for all the world like they posed for American Gothic.

Nobody's going to like what they see in the pictures anyway. Aunt Martha'll look too fat (probably because she *is* too fat), little Bruno (Is there such a thing as a Jewish kid named *Bruno?*) will be caught pulling his cousin's hair, and Grandpa Sam will look old because at eighty-four there's no way he's going to look young.

So why waste a thousand dollars on still photos?

You don't have to, plain and simple.

There are three ways of dealing with the problem:

1. Get your second cousin who thinks he's a hot-shot photographer to borrow your Canon AE-1 Program (or use his own camera) and you spring for the film; or

2. Buy a series of $9.95 instant one-time cameras. If you by a bunch of them, you can probably get them for $7.95 each at Price-Costco, Sam's Club, etc. Your guests will get an extra thrill by being their own "candid" photograpers. Just make sure the cameras are somehow nailed to the table so some guest won't "accidentally" take one home; or

3. Go back to the local college, the photography class this time, and try to work out the same deal you did for the videotaping. As an added incentive to the photographer, you should note that for whatever reason, people love to have individual, family, or "couple" shots, no matter the event. The Hawaiian and Caribbean hotel-restaurants learned this long ago. Resort guests figure they're paying for a meal and a good time, so what's the extra five bucks if you have an individual picture? I'll tell you what's the extra five bucks— money in *your* pocket.

With the advent of the "one hour photo" stores, you don't even have to suffer through the funny-colored Polaroid shots. Your guests can have *real* pictures—take-home souvenirs of Herschel's Bar Mitzvah. And you split the net with the photographer.

$ **11** $

THE "THEME" BAR MITZVAH

This isn't strictly a money-saving thing. Rather it's something that will make Herschel's Bar Mitzvah special and memorable.

In larger cities, it has become fashionable to have the entire event coordinated around a "Theme." It can be as simple as "Pretty in Pink," with everything color-coordinated (napkins, tablecloths, programs, pink-colored hot dogs (*ugh!*), dishes, tuxedos)—which doesn't work very well at a *Bar* Mitzvah—or as elaborate as the imagination allows. Things like "Safari!" (Sure! How many Masai tribesmen do you know who celebrate Bar Mitzvahs?); "Disneyland on Parade" (At least Mickey Mouse wears a *Yarmulke*); or "Teen Idols" (That'll work if you spell the last name Spring*stein*).

But, like anything else, the more elaborate you get, the more money you put out. Savings time!

Here are some grand suggestions based upon "different" themes that I've not yet seen:

1. **Old Timer's Night:** The Bar Mitzvah centers on a 'thirties or 'forties theme. Find out if there are any *old* musicians in your town who'd like to try out for stardom one last time. Actually, even though this saves money and they'd probably play for free or very little, this is one of the real *Mitzvahs*. You make everyone happy, particularly the retirees who all-too-often feel they've been put out to pasture.

2. **The Gong Show:** Every town has its one-man-band, it's slightly off-center trainer of mongrel dogs, pigeons or white mice, or the next Maria Callas. Not only that, every event has at least one—more likely ten—obnoxious relatives who really think they're the next best thing to the *real* stars. It costs nothing to announce in advance that Herschel's Bar Mitzvah will be centered around a talent contest.

CAUTION: You could get too many entrants. After all, a theme is just window dressing, you don't want it to overshadow Herschel.

SOLUTION: If too many people want to perform, you could charge each contestant an entry fee for the privilege. (Hmmm. Now that's another idea for making a profit. Why not charge an entry fee anyway? You can give the winner a cheap prize and still make a nifty little bundle.)

As you can see, it's all in what psychologists call the "mind set." If you've come this far in the book, you're probably even coming up with new and original money-saving/money-making ideas of your own. It is the purpose of any good book to educate, to challenge, to stimulate thinking. However, if you think I'm going to pay you anything for your own original suggestions, guess again. This book is *my* money-making project.

3. **Animals on Parade:** Here's a good deed, a money saver, and something that will make at least some of your guests remember Herschel's Bar Mitzvah for a *long* time.

The local SPCA or animal shelter is always looking for good homes for unwanted dogs, cats, and assorted four-legged beasties. Invite them to bring an assortment of such pets—properly tended, of course—to the party. Your guests can select a pet and go home with a true party favor. Try to make sure the SPCA brings animals that are housebroken.

4. **High School High Jinks:** Hey, hey, take it away, get that ball and fight! This can work, but it has to be done carefully. That means

you invite the local cheerleading squad or baton twirler's club to perform *after* the meal has been served. This is a variation on the *Gong Show* theme, but have you ever seen a baton twirler that doesn't want to perform *anywhere*, any time?

By now you've seen that almost all these cost-free schemes center on inviting the types of performers who hunger after the exposure they wouldn't ordinarily get. Thus, it's an intelligent idea to concentrate on those types who would not usually get the chance to showcase their talents. You might consider the following:

1. Barbershop quartets.
2. Musical saw or glass-bottle players.
3. Poetry readers (I'd be careful here. They get awfully weird sometimes.)
4. Amateur magicians.
5. Amateur ventriloquists.
6. Accordionists whose specialty is "Lady of Spain."
7. Bagpipers.
8. Tuba soloists.
9. Those ubiquitous, pestiferous mimes that inhabit any street corner in any big city and follow you mercilessly about trying to demonstrate in five hundred ways—without ever saying a word, of course—that they want and crave appreciation, love, and, if you have some spare change, money!
10. Any other specialty where the first reaction the audience will have is, *"OH, MY GOD!"*

$ 12 $

FOOD AND DRINK

We've saved the ticklish part of money management until we got this far along and your mind is fine-tuned to deal with the cold, hard fact that virtually no one gives away food and very few people give away drinks.

As usual, we attack the easy problems first and move from there to the ones that require greater creativity.

Jews don't ordinarily drink hard liquor. That's good from a standpoint of logistics as well as saving money. Wine, however, is considered a "must" at a Bar Mitzvah.

There are several alternatives.

The first, best, and least likely (unless you live in California or parts of New York or anywhere else there's a burgeoning wine industry) is to try to have a winery or even a liquor store sponsor a wine-tasting as an adjunct to Herschel's Bar Mitzvah. If they agree to it, you give them a corner of the room where the bar might otherwise be, big signs, a whole glitzy send-off. (If they go for this, you might consider this as an alternate theme—"A Trip to the Wine Country.") They supply all the wine, and, hopefully, they'll sell some as well. Don't even think of trying to split profits with these guys. They're defraying a major expense—a big ticket item—and they know it. Hopefully they'll bring crackers, cheese, nuts, and other *noshes* (snacks) that will help cut down on your own food bill.

Failing that, there are still viable alternatives.

One of God's greatest and most recent inventions is the discount warehouse—Price Costco, (Jewish-owned, incidentally), Sam's Club, Liquor Barn, and the like. These places specialize in odd lot wine. The only size bottle they have is huge—a single bottle provides for ten people—and they always come in packs of two, held together by shrink-wrap plastic so strong you can cut steel with it. You'd never use such a magnum at home unless you had a Herschel's Bar Mitzvah-sized party at your house.

Also, you don't want to buy a case of wine—twenty-four bottles. You never use them all, they're a pain in the *tuches* (south end of a donkey going north) to return, and they end up lying around the house or the garage until Herschel and his friends get a bit older, discover what alcohol is all about, and start experimenting. Not a good idea.

At Price Costco two bottles cost about ten bucks. And they're "name" brand wines. So for a hundred people you can figure about Sixty dollars, right? Wrong. Your goal is to save money anywhere, any time. So you engage in "Give a *mitzvah*, get a *mitzvah*."

You look over the list of events coming up at the synagogue. Most likely, there will be at least three Bar Mitzvahs within two months of the one you're planning. If not, you can always return to your friend, Pastor Martin, and see if he's got any events coming up.

You then pass the word of this miraculous place where they can buy wine much cheaper than at a liquor store. It's called Price Costco (etc).

We'll assume these folks listen to what you say and are properly appreciative for the information you've given them. And that they immediately go out and, lured by the low prices, buy too much wine. (After all, it would be the biggest embarrassment to be caught with not enough wine.)

We'll also assume that either they—or their guests—will immediately break open the plastic binding which holds the two bottles together, thus making return for a refund impossible.

Two days after their event, picture the following telephone conversation, initiated by you, of course.

YOU: "Judy? Abby Adams here. I heard your son's Bar Mitzvah was the greatest event in years. I'm just dying to hear about it, 'cause Herschel's is only a month away."

OTHER WOMAN: "Oh, Abby, it was terrific. I just wish you could have been there. You know, only one thing went a little wrong. We took your advice and went to Price Costco. Thanks again for that. But when we got there, the prices were so reasonable and Fred and I were so worried we wouldn't have enough wine that we bought a little too much."

YOU: "That's no problem at all, Judy. Price Costco's real good about taking the stuff back. Heck, I'd planned on going shopping there myself this Thursday afternoon. If you'd like, I'll take it back for you."

O.W.: "That's awfully kind of you, Abby, but the problem is someone broke those plastic binders apart and you can't expect the store to take them back. I'm afraid we're stuck with ten bottles of wine that we'll never use."

YOU: "Gosh, Judy, that is a shame. You can always wrap them up and give them as gifts, can't you?"

O.W.: "We could, but we probably never will. That's the kind of stuff that just takes up room in the cupboard until it rots. Say, your Herschel's Bar Mitzvah's just around the corner. Could you use some of the wine we've got left over?"

YOU: "I don't know, Judy. We've picked out this special brand my husband likes and you know how men are about their pride and taste. I think I'd better wait until I talk with him. What kind of wine is it, anyway?"

O.W.: "Sebastiani Chardonnay. Really good stuff."

YOU: "Oh, darn! I'd hoped you'd have said (insert any other brand you can think of). I'm so sorry, Judy."

O.W.: "Are you sure you couldn't use the Sebastiani? Listen, I could give you a really good deal on it. Say thirty dollars for the ten bottles? Half price."

YOU: "Well...I don't know. I sure don't want to cause a family argument. What would Fred say?"

O.W.: "He'd be glad to get rid of the stuff. Listen, Abby, take all the bottles for twenty-five dollars, ok?"

YOU: "Well, Judy, I sure don't want to sound like a *schnorrer*..."

O.W.: "Please, Abby, you'll be doing me a favor."

YOU: (Yielding, but very reluctantly). "All right, but my husband's going to be furious. I'll just try to deal with it as best I can."

Voila! A dollar saved is a dollar earned, and you've just saved thirty-five of them. Or, to put it another way, more than a fifty percent savings in addition to the fifty percent or so off retail which you would have paid at Price Costco. Wine is a big ticket item. At less than fifty dollars for the affair, you've done yourself proud.

The non-alcoholic drinks? Obviously, if you're going to use soft drinks, you use the kind that sponsored the invitations. The first line of attack here is to try to push things a little bit by letting the sponsor company know you intend to use their product and to ask how many cans or bottles would they be willing to give you for the celebration.

Failing that, see if Judy-from-the-wine has any soft drinks left. If that doesn't work, you might have to make your Thursday afternoon trip to Price Costco after all. But while you're there, buy only *one* case of your sponsor's product (to salve your conscience). As for the rest, Price Costco most likely has fifty-gallon drums (or a similar size) of

Hawaiian Punch concentrate for $5.97 (Did you ever notice their prices are not only low, they're weird?). So it will be soft drinks for the very few, but a punch bowl for the masses.

All right, now comes the point we've been dreading throughout this book, the big-buck-gobbler, the reason for the entire celebration (particularly if you're Jewish): **FOOD.**

The best possible way to handle this is, unfortunately, looked upon as "*grob*" (declassé). It involves a lot of *chutzpah,* and normally it doesn't work at all. But it might, and you've really got nothing to lose, because if it does pan out, it's like finding gold.

You arrange a meeting of Socially Prominent Ladies in the Jewish community (note the proper capitalization), particularly younger ones, even more particularly those who've got a Bar or Bat Mitzvah coming up after yours. Ideally, it can be brought up at a Sisterhood, Hadassah, or Jewish Women's International (they used to call themselves B'nai B'rith Women) meeting. I leave the wording up to you. It's concept that counts.

Your opening salvo should be,

> "What ever happened to the good old Jewish theme of community and togetherness? You know, Jews helping other Jews, making a social event a real *community* event? Nowadays everyone tries to outdo everyone else, spending tens of thousands of dollars for a Bar Mitzvah, and for what? No matter how good the food, it's gone from your body in two days anyway, so what's the big deal? Frankly, I'm spending thousands of dollars just like the rest of you. Not that I can't afford it (God forbid!) but it seems such a waste. Why, when I was a little girl, families got together and everyone brought one of their specialties. It wasn't like a pot luck, exactly, because every woman who came could point with pride to what she'd brought to make the event so special."

Ideally, someone will pick up the ball and run with the idea. Of course, you don't want the idea to be picked up by *everyone*, because you're not that community minded that you want the entire Jewish community to attend Herschel's Bar Mitzvah. I mean, could you imagine what an incredible bunch of guests you'd have running around?

You want *some* of the "girls" to pick it up. Just not that many.

There are three directions this can take. Focus on the first two, because they're positive:

1. Several women will volunteer to form a committee to make sure you don't have to worry about the food, it'll all be taken care of; or

2. Several women will form a committee to go to the men's club and get them to take care of things so you don't have to worry about the food.

Incidentally, to make this idea work, you have to be the *first* in your group to suggest it. After two or three times, there'll be far fewer volunteers and the men's club will say, "We've already done our share."

The third alternative is that you'll get turned down. Let's face it, win some, lose some.

If you've lost this one, the name of the game is to minimize your losses. Early on, we've decided that the synagogue is much better, much more harmonious, much more in keeping with the symbolism of the event (translation: much cheaper) than a hotel or restaurant. So now the question is: buffet or served meal?

Initially, you may think the sit-down meal is best. After all, there'll be no wasted food, people will eat what they're served, and that will be that. Why should you lay out a buffet? These *chazzers* (big eaters) will eat more than they would normally eat, and what they don't consume they'll wrap in tin foil (have you ever known a Jew to call it "aluminum foil?") and take home with them.

This is small thinking.

There's an old saying: Those who feed the masses eat with the classes. Those who feed the classes eat with the masses.

McDonald's knows that saying very well. So do Sizzler, Wendy's, Burger King, and others who pride themselves on having a table where you can pick up "All you can eat." Peoples' eyes are invariably bigger than their stomachs. More important, particularly with women at an event, you can count on two facts:

1. A woman is not going to let another human being see her stuffing herself.
2. A woman is not going to let another human being see her husband stuffing himself.

The old "*Ess, ess, mein kindt*," (Eat, eat my darling child!) that Jewish mothers are so famous for applies to *sons, not husbands!* (Another reason to invite as few kids as you can get away with to the event).

So how do you work it?

The best (*i.e.* least expensive) way of doing this, is to get several girlfriends over (you can always use your husband in a pinch) to chop lettuce, cut fruit, loan you trays, and lay out cold cuts and cheese (separate trays, of course, we wouldn't think of serving meat and milk products together) on those platters. This cuts out the middleman. All you have to do is buy bread, meat, cheese, pickles, etc.—you can always refrigerate what's left.

If you want to go "that extra step"—you've seen what I mean, where they have a lovely, carved-up whole salmon surrounded by cucumber curlicues—that's easy enough to do. Have hubby wrap a whole fish in tin foil and barbecue it the night before. Salmon is delicious when you add dill weed, rosemary, a little wine, a little lemon, some onions and a small can of tomato sauce, wrap the whole thing and cook it about half-an-hour on a side. (Now you've got an extra reason to buy this book. Two volumes in one—a money saver and a mini-cookbook).

Bagels, rye bread, cream cheese are not horribly expensive. Lox is horribly expensive. Barbecued salmon is every bit as good, at one-fourth the price.

The last thing you want to serve is a hot meal, but if you absolutely must, roast a couple of briskets (Dry onion soup mix, garlic powder, tomato sauce, sliced onions, a little salt, wrap in foil, roast in the oven for 1½ hours at 325 degrees, unwrap and cook for the last 30-45 minutes), and slice them.

Potato salad and cole slaw may be a bit of an expense, but let the deli do it. It's too much of a hassle and a mess to make it yourself.

You can probably get out for under two hundred dollars, and even that's stretching it. Consider that caterers charge anywhere from fifteen to twenty-five dollars per person.

```
100 people, $20 average per person . . . . . . . $ 2,000
Less cost to lay out the spread yourself . . . . . . ( 200)
Net $aving$. . . . . . . . . . . . . . . . . . . . . . . . . $ 1,800
```

So much for savings. The profit will come on the day of the event, provided you have the *chutzpah* to pull it off.

Incidentally, this *chutzpah*—if it catches on—could work a salutary effect of *T'z'dakah*—and actually help people!

Here's how it works:

When guests get to the buffet line, they start gathering their food. Eventually, they come to the end of the line and then they see it! A large food scale. A cash register. And a discreet sign that says, "Perform a real mitzvah! Weigh your own meal. We suggest you contribute $1.00 per ounce. More than half of the money you voluntarily contribute for your meal will go to (name the charity of your choice). We accept Visa, MasterCard, Discover Card and American Express." (Incidentally, what is now so highly praised as

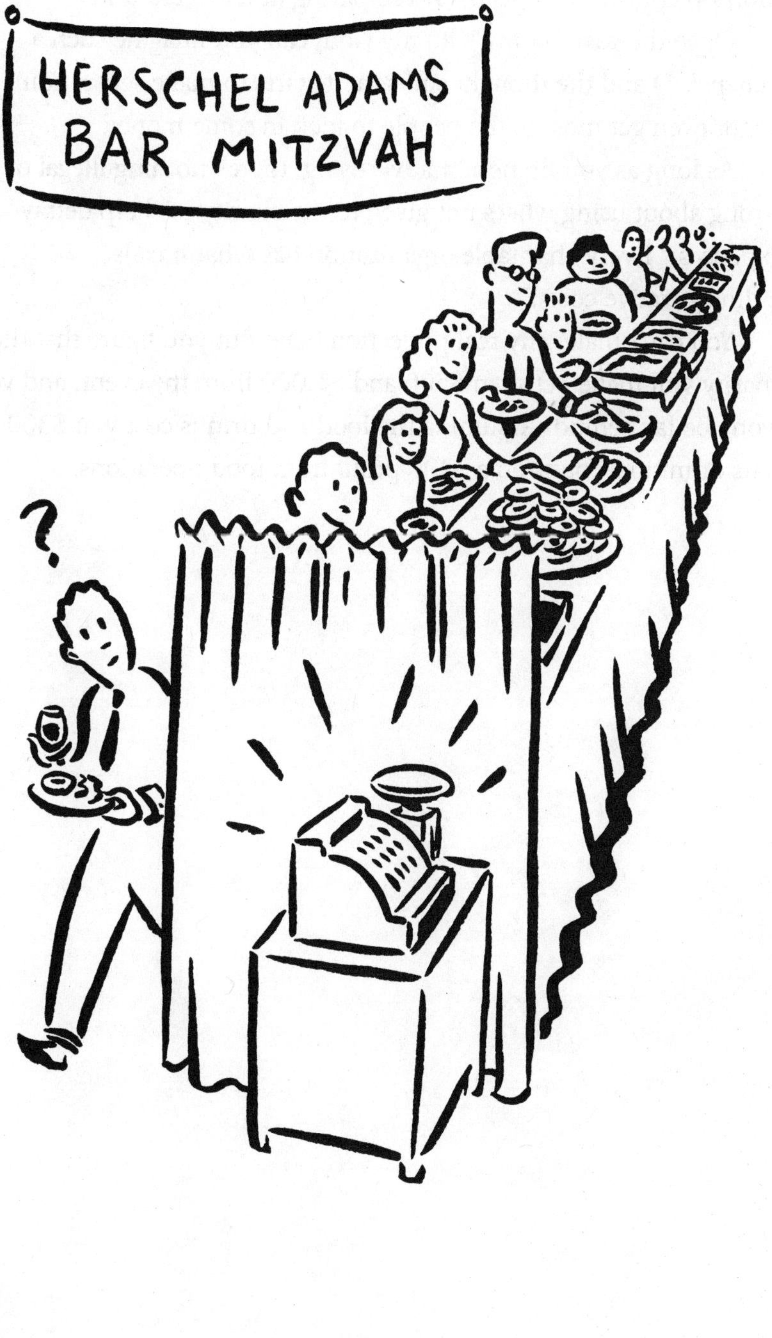
HERSCHEL ADAMS
BAR MITZVAH
?

"nouvelle cuisine" is exactly the same thing that used to be called "portion control" by cheap, cheese-paring hotel restaurants).

Once the gasps stop ("Oh, my God, can you imagine such a *chutzpah?*") and the thought sinks in, it starts to make sense. You might even get most of the people to kick in some money.

As long as you do honest advertising, there's nothing illegal or wrong about using what's not given to the charity to "help defray expenses." Every charitable organization has what it calls "administrative costs."

You can't make any real projection here. But you figure that the charity will make between $500 and $1,000 from the event, and you won't be far behind. Assuming the food and drinks cost you $300, plus or minus, count on a $200 profit from food operations.

$ 13 $

CUSTOM YARMULKES

If you really want to go first class, it is *de rigueur* that you have custom-made yarmulkes—*kipot* they call them nowadays. (For our Christian readers, these are the small skullcaps traditionally worn by Jews. For the education of everyone, they are meant to symbolize the borderline which divides heaven and earth, God and mankind). You've seen them before, red or purple-colored velvet that invariably say something like, "Herschel's Bar Mitzvah, January 15, ___." Did you ever notice that they never have the kid's last name? I don't know why, they just never do.

Expensive little fellows, these. As in two dollars fifty-cents per. Figure an expenditure of two hundred fifty dollars. Also figure the yarmulke makers aren't going to go along with "sponsoring" the job by putting their name in the lining. Some unscrupulous ones do that anyway, without asking.

Time to hunt up a sponsor again. You've hit the kosher butcher, the dry cleaner and the real estate agents. (Although you should try to hit real estate agents and insurance agents again, they're always good for this).

Believe it or not, as stingy as they usually are, lawyers are prime candidates for *yarmulke* sponsorship. You see, for many years attorneys (they like to call themselves that; sometimes they even throw in "attorney and counselor at law") were prohibited from

advertising. Some still consider themselves "above that kind of thing" since law is "a profession, not a business." (Oh, yeah? See how many lawyers will take on your case simply for "professional pride").

Thus, they have to find a vehicle to "advertise without advertising." If you think that's double-talk, just try and pin a lawyer down to anything. The perfect solution is the *yarmulke*. Discreet. Dignified. Always there. Doesn't tear like a business card. And do you know of anyone who's going to risk the wrath of heaven by throwing one away?

Kiwanis, Rotary, Lions, etc. is another good bet. Remember, their programs are geared toward *Youth.*

The intelligent Bar Mitzvah planner will take all these things into consideration. Irrespective of what any sponsors may try to foist off on the public, their motivating force is greed. Yours should be, too. Within reasonable limits, of course.

Five hundred four dollars is the perfect amount.

In Hebrew "*Chai*" is a magic number. It's the number eighteen, and the word just happens to mean "life" as well. (Thus *L'Chaim*—To Life!) That's why, a lot of times, you'll see contributions in synagogue made in multiples of *Chai*—eighteen.

Eighteen times eighteen equals Five Hundred Four Dollars.

A perfect sales pitch for the perfect symbol of the Bar Mitzvah!

One caution, however. The attorney or other sponsor should be limited to one or two lines. After all, you don't want to spend more on the *yarmulkes* than you absolutely have to.

$ 14 $

OPTIONAL SCHEME: GIFT GIVING MADE EASY

You may rest assured that in the ordinary Bar Mitzvah event, Herschel may expect a dozen fountain or ball point pens (old jokes never die!), some Israeli bonds, miscellaneous ties, cufflinks, gift certificates to a record store or book store, and that greatest-of-all deceptions, U.S. Savings Bonds. I don't say "deceptive" because of what they are. U.S. Savings Bonds are a fine and worthwhile investment. I say deceptive because these bonds are printed very cleverly: The denomination printed on the bond is the amount the bond *will be worth at maturity.*

It's come to be a nice trick to buy a Bar or Bat Mitzvah a one hundred dollar bond. It looks big, it looks wonderful, and it only costs fifty dollars. So it looks like you're giving one hundred dollars, but you're not really. This deception doesn't work anymore, 'cause sooner or later everyone gets the idea and starts doing the same thing.

Now, obviously, you are not giving a Bar Mitzvah so the kid can get cufflinks and fountain pens. One of the main reasons for throwing this bash is to put a little money in the kitty for Herschel's college—even though you know he's going to get a full scholarship.

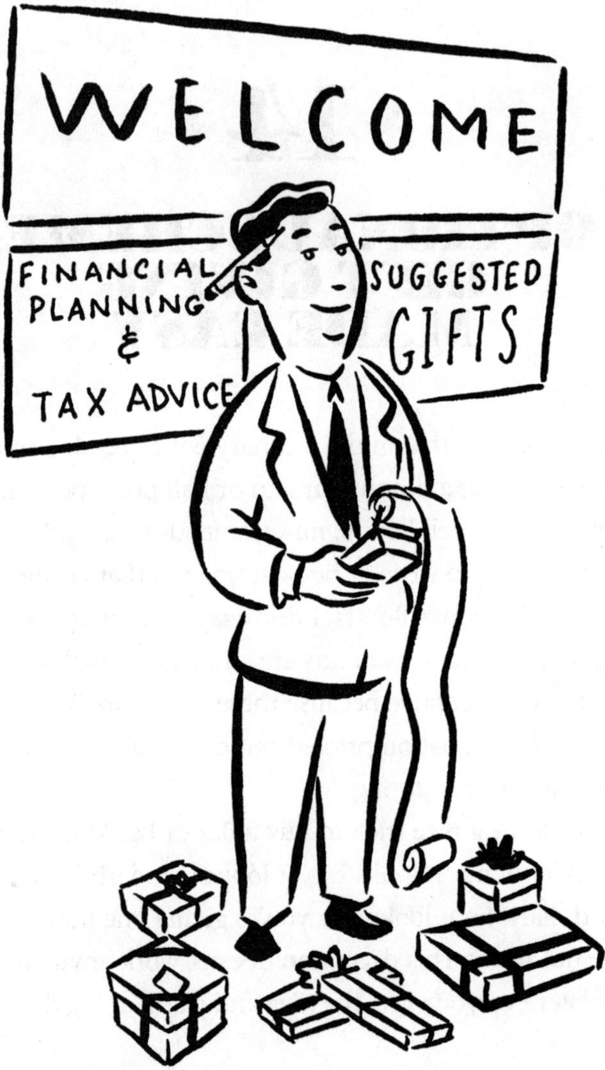
WELCOME
FINANCIAL PLANNING & TAX ADVICE
SUGGESTED GIFTS

The time has come to stop the double-talk and subterfuge and come straight to the point. Let it be known throughout the community (diplomatically, of course, although how you can *schnorr* (beg) diplomatically may be a problem unless you're a born salesperson) that Herschel has plenty of cufflinks, ties, pens, and "things" (in the event of a Bat Mitzvah, let it be known that Debbie has all the necklaces with Jewish stars on them she'll ever need, thank you), and that he truly would like to keep it simple and just get money—for his university education, of course.

The announcement is all well and good, but then you have to rely on the voluntary generosity of your guests. Historically, you can figure on Herschel getting back in monetary gifts about a third of what it costs you to put on the Bar Mitzvah (assuming you haven't used the money-saving/money-making ideas in this book).

Much more scientific—indeed painless—is to let another word go out. You will have a "financial counselor" at the Bar Mitzvah who will assist each guest in making an "appropriate" gift. The advisor will demonstrate to each guest how "more is less"—that is, the tax savings to the donor in making an ever larger gift to the honoree. The counselor will be seated immediately outside the *shul*, cleverly disguised as a greeter who checks names off as people come in. He takes a little more time than usual, indicating to them that he is in charge of receiving the gifts on Herschel's behalf—"you wouldn't want your gift to get lost, would you?" He then discusses with them the tax advantages of a generous donation, offering to review the donor's income tax return, if necessary, to demonstrate exactly how much the guest could save by making a generous, tax-deductible gift for Youth.

Some people may think this is a fairly *grob* way of doing things. Thus, you might carefully consider variations on the "greeter." He could be at the cash register for the food, or he might even be in the middle of the dance floor (although that's a poor and unsafe place to be—either people don't go onto the dance floor, or when they do their gyrations are certain to cause injury).

Just remember, the sour taste of momentary embarrassment is more than offset by the fact that five years down the line Herschel's gifts, drawing interest the whole time, will make college, a car, or whatever, that much less of a burden on you.

$ **15** $

LOOK BACK IN JOY!

I'm sure that there are several ideas I've not explored, contingencies which may exist, little differences here and there which will personalize your own event. But these are small matters which you may have to work out yourself—or wait for the second edition of this book—and I hope that by this time I've educated you sufficiently that you can improvise if the emergency arises.

Now it comes time to see exactly what buying this book has saved you. We do a side-by-side comparison:

	Before you bought this book	After you bought this book
Invitations	$ 300	$ -0-
Postage	150	-0-
Return postage/envelopes	150	-0-
Synagogue rent	150	Net -0-
Social hall	500	500 but includes furniture and janitorial
Food/Caterer	6,000	+ 300
Band	1,500	30 but you get *two* live bands and a disk jockey
Flowers	250	+ 100
Decorations	250	-0-
Wine/drinks	1,500	Included in food
Rabbi	50	Duplicate gift
Cantor	50	-0-
Furniture rent	100	-0-
Janitorial	150	-0-
Video recording	500	-0-
Photographer	1,000	-0-
Programs	minimal	+ 3,320.50
Napkins, matchbooks	250	-0-
Custom yarmulkes	250	+ 254
Sleeping pills during planning	100	-0-
Cost of this book	-0-	9.95
Total:	**$ 13,200**	**($ 3,434.55)!***

* That's *negative* $3,434.55, translation: *profit!*

This does not take into consideration residual program sales, residual videotape sales or residual photograph sales.

The total savings, including money you made and money you *didn't* spend comes to *$16,634.55!!!* You have not only survived, you have *profited* from your son's Bar Mitzvah, your daughter's Bat

Mitzvah, or any other event where you were expected to pay the bill. *Mazel tov!*

If you figure I'll make at least that—and hopefully many times more—for having written this book, but that *I'll* have to take the verbal abuse that's sure to come from virtually everyone (My mother and sister already said *they* don't like it and how could I have said such things in a book?), which of us really came out ahead?

❧ Almost The End ❦

NOTE

Now that the fun-and-profit portion of the book is over, I'd like to take this opportunity to really wish you *Mazel Tov* on your wonderful event. Regardless of whether you abide by the instructions in this book or otherwise, you really are perpetuating a belief and a morality base that has lasted more than 5,700 years. My family and I wish you much *naches.*

Now it's

THE END

Marvin Shapiro is the pseudonymn of a

nationally known trial attorney, writer, and vice president

of his congregation.

He lives in a small community on the central

California coast.

"This hilarious satire on one of the great events of Jewish life pokes not-so-gentle, perhaps well-deserved fun at excesses that all-too-often drown out the important meaning of this most special day. Bravo!"

> – Rabbi Sanford M. Shapero
> former Regional Director
> Union of American Hebrew Congregations

"How to Survive—And Profit From Your Son's Bar Mitzvah is proof positive that you don't have to be Jewish to enjoy a good laugh. This book can be applied to situations all over the world, whatever the religion or event.... And they say I write strange things..."

> – Gary Jennings
> Best-selling Author of
> *Aztec, The Journeyer, Spangle, Raptor*

"This man ought to be locked up...in a room, on a stage, where he can bring laughter to hundreds, perhaps thousands. A joyous journey through what can be a torturous experience. A unique and laugh-filled Bar Mitzvah gift—preferably before the big day arrives."

> – Rabbi Norman T. Mendel
> Pastoral Director
> City of Hope National Medical Center

"Thought provoking.... Fun. Ditzy, but fun..."

> – Bruce Greenbaum, Rabbi,
> Charles Beren, President
> Congregation Beth Israel
> Carmel, California

"Oy! And to think my son wrote something like this..."

> – Trudy Gerstl
> Former Regional President
> B'nai B'rith Women (Jewish Women International)